GROWING UP IN SHAWNEE, OKLAHOMA, among a host of grandmothers and aunties, Loretta Barrett Oden learned the lessons and lore of Potawatomi cooking, along with those of her father's family, whose ancestors arrived on the Mayflower. This rich cultural blend came to bear in the iconic restaurant she opened in Santa Fe, the Corn Dance Café, where many of the dishes in this book had their debut, setting Oden on her path to fame as one of the most influential Native chefs in the nation, a leader in the new Indigenous food movement, and, with her Emmy Award–winning PBS series, *Seasoned with Spirit: A Native Cook's Journey*, a cross-cultural ambassador for First American cuisine.

Corn Dance: Inspired First American Cuisine tells the story of Oden's journey and of the dishes she created along the way. Alongside recipes that combine the flavors of her Oklahoma upbringing and Indigenous heritage with the Southwest flair of her Santa Fe restaurant, Oden offers edifying observations about ingredients and cooking culture. These and many practical words of wisdom about using the fruits of the forest, stream, or plain accompany Loretta's insights on everything from the dubious provenance of fry bread to the Potawatomi legend behind the Three Sisters—corn, beans, and squash, the namesake ingredients of Three Sisters and Friends Salad, served now at Thirty Nine Restaurant at First Americans Museum in Oklahoma City, where Oden is the Chef Consultant.

LORETTA BARRETT ODEN is a renowned, Emmy Award–winning Native American chef, food historian, lecturer, and member of the Citizen Potawatomi Nation. She lives in Oklahoma City.

BETH DOOLEY is a James Beard Award–winning food journalist and holds an Endowed Chair at Minnesota Institute for Sustainable Agriculture. She is the author of eight cookbooks, including (with Sean Sherman) *The Sioux Chef's Indigenous Kitchen*.

"Wonderful stories and recipes for food I can attest to being satisfyingly delicious!"

Wes Studi (Cherokee Nation)
award-winning actor, musician, and artist

"Loretta is a true inspiration and role model. Years before anyone else, she broke new ground and opened up new paths for what is possible when she brought Indigenous foods into a restaurant setting with her Corn Dance Café. I am proud to call Loretta a friend and mentor, and am so excited to see her stories, recipes, and philosophy in the form of this beautiful cookbook! Pilamayeyelo, Loretta, for all you have done!"

Sean Sherman (Oglala Lakota)
Founder, The Sioux Chef / Owamni / NATIFS / Indigenous Food Lab

"*Corn Dance* is an irresistible invitation into Potawatomi chef Loretta Oden's kitchen. For Oden we need a bigger word than "chef." She is an artist, a renowned leader in the movement to revitalize Indigenous foods, a creator, a rememberer, and a storyteller. She tells stories with food—stories about the land, gardens, history, family, life—and helps us savor it all. I want to sit around her table with the grandmothers, shelling beans and shucking corn while she stirs up a new sauce that brings it all together, with flavors and ingredients from the four directions. We are in her debt for this bighearted book, which is sweet, savory, and wise."

Robin Wall Kimmerer (Citizen Patowatomi)
author of *Braiding Sweetgrass: Indigenous Wisdom,
Scientific Knowledge, and the Teachings of Plants*

"Through her knowledge, food, and activism, Loretta has blazed a trail for Indigenous women like me who seek to revive our connection to our land and our food as a way to heal in all the ways that word intends. With *Corn Dance* and her recipes using traditional ingredients, Loretta is inviting a larger community to know the abundance of our ancestors so that we may forge a better future for our Earth and its people."

Crystal Wahpepah (Kickapoo Tribe of Oklahoma)
Chef-Owner of Wahpepah's Kitchen

"Loretta Barrett Oden is a legend. A trailblazer in the field of Indigenous cuisine, she remains an influential voice in the food sovereignty movement today. *Corn Dance* is a culmination of her lifetime of travels through Indian Country. The stories and recipes contained here present a balance of traditional ancestral dishes and the chef's own original creations within the context of a life lived with and *for* the Native community."

Nico Albert Williams (Cherokee Nation)
Founder and Executive Director of Burning Cedar Sovereign
Wellness and Executive Chef of Burning Cedar Sovereign Kitchen

"Loretta's enchanting storytelling and delightful recipes bring us together to celebrate the deeply complex cultural history of our First American relatives, bridging our modern world with the foods and medicines that have healed our lands and our bodies for centuries. This book satisfies the hungry historian and is practical for any home cook. *Corn Dance* offers us a way to connect directly with the abundance of nature and the sacred foods of First Americans."

Caesaré Assad
Founder and Food System Consultant, Centipede Collective

"*Corn Dance* contains recipes to last a lifetime, each one mouthwatering and inspirational. Loretta's whole life is an inspiration. Her Corn Dance Café broke so many barriers for women and for Native cooks. This is much more than a cookbook: you will feel her spirit and cook with joy."

Pati Martinson
Cofounder and Codirector, Taos County Economic Development Corp

CORN DANCE

CORN DANCE

Inspired First American Cuisine

Loretta Barrett Oden
with Beth Dooley

UNIVERSITY OF OKLAHOMA PRESS : NORMAN

Photos on pages 12–13, 38–39, 46, 66–67, 72, 102–3, 127, 138–39, and 151 by Ethan Stewart, OU Marketing and Communications. Photos on pages 53, 78, 108, 123, 127, 132–33, 138, 175, 200, and 213 from iStock/Getty Images. All other photos, unless otherwise noted, are by Metta Nielsen (copyright © 2024 by Metta Nielsen).

Library of Congress Cataloging in Publication Control Number:
ISBN 978-0-8061-9078-5 (hardcover)

The paper in this book meets the guidelines for permanence and durability of the Committee on Production Guidelines for Book Longevity of the Council on Library Resources, Inc. ∞

1 2 3 4 5 6 7 8 9 10

To my boys, Clay and Craig—my joy and inspiration

CONTENTS

NOTES FROM LORETTA'S KITCHEN

Acknowledgments

First and foremost, my thanks go to my boys, Clay and Craig, to whom this book is dedicated. I start with them and their Dad, Jerry, because they always ate what I cooked—the good, the not so good, and the experiments. They were my sweet, 'cause-they-were-always-hungry Guinea pigs. They rarely complained, and over the years, my cooking improved. They, along with my precious grandchildren, have helped me to develop and hone my culinary knowledge and skills.

For help in bringing this book to life, I offer undying gratitude, first, to consummate food writer and cook Beth Dooley and also to editors Alessandra Jacobi Tamulevich and Steven Baker, freelance copyeditor Pam Price, designer Tony Roberts, and all the others at (or with) OU Press. Thanks for your unflagging support and hard work throughout this process. You've all been amazing!

My cooking, like nearly everyone else's, begins at home. From a very large and diverse family came multiple influences—Mom, Grandmas, Great-Grandmas, and Aunties, as well as more than a few of the menfolk. Their knowledge and wisdom are firmly imbedded in all that I do.

I have also eaten at many wonderful restaurants over the years, but it was not until I moved away from Oklahoma and traveled specifically to research Indigenous foods that my chef's mind exploded. Indigenous food and foodways became a true passion, and even now, hardly a day passes that I don't discover something new, often accompanied by laughter, dance, song, or tears of joy!

So many, many amazing people in so many places have generously shared their extraordinary knowledge of food, seeds, planting, growing, harvesting, cooking, and celebration. The enormous bounty and diversity of our foodways inhere in those teachings, feeding and defining our very cultures.

I cannot begin to name all those who have guided and taught me through these many decades. Please know that not naming someone here does not mean that a single person or entity is forgotten. Your names and your gifts to me are indelibly etched into my heart and my spirit forever. You, each and every one, have honored me and tasked me to carry and share your words and deeds throughout my days on Turtle Island.

Migwech.

Introduction

I was born in Shawnee, Oklahoma, blessed with amazing Grandmothers, Great-Grandmothers, Aunties, Great-Aunties, and a beautiful Mother who taught me to garden and cook. I am proud of my origins as a member of the Potawatomi people. My relatives were relocated from the Great Lakes region to Mayetta, Kansas, with the Prairie Band Potawatomi. My tribe split from the Prairie Band and moved to Indian Territory, known today as Oklahoma. In later years, our tribal chairman, my brother Rocky Barrett, changed the name to Citizen Potawatomi Nation. Oklahoma, home to thirty-nine tribes, is truly the "Melting Pot of Indian Country."

My Potawatomi Grandmother Peltier, my Mom's Mom, had a profound influence on my life. She took my hand from babyhood forward, and her teachings are woven into my psyche and spirit. We sang as we planted beans, corn, and squash (the Three Sisters); we sang as our crops grew and we touched them tenderly, praying for rain and sun; and at harvest, we gave thanks to Mother Earth for her bounty.

In the spring, we gathered young poke, lambsquarters, dandelion, and other wild greens, then the wild blackberries and strawberries and those luscious first tomatoes. We fished and gigged frogs, a must in the hot summers, and we devoured huge watermelons and sweet cantaloupes, their sticky juices running down our arms. Later in the summer and into the fall, we collected wild possum grapes, sand plums, pecans, and walnuts, as well as the native persimmons, but only after the first frost. Take a bite of one before that and you'd really pucker up, a mistake you'd make only once! But, when ripe, oh, how rich and luscious the delicious persimmon pudding and bread! The "men folk," as Grandma Peltier called them, went hunting for deer, squirrel, possum, raccoon, and wild fowl—turkey, duck, goose, quail, prairie chicken, pheasant, and dove. In earlier times, the buffalo roamed.

Grandma Peltier showed me the moon's ways and told me the stories of the constellations as we lay on the homemade quilts spread out in her yard looking into starry sky. She recognized every bird's song and explained night

(*Above, left*) The Peltier side of my family, all Citizen Potawatomi, near Oklahoma City, in the 1940s. From left: Aunt Mildred Peltier Schimmel, Great Uncle Arthur Peltier, Loretta Anne Barrett, Great Aunt Pauline Bourassa Peltier, Cousin Mildred Ann Schimmel, John Adams (Rocky) Barrett, Cousin Richard Schimmel, Grandmother Bourassa Peltier, Robert Schimmel, Aunt Ruby Peltier Erwin, and Grandfather Oliver Albert Peltier. Courtesy Citizen Potawatomi Nation Cultural Center. (*Above, right*) My Mother, Annetta Mae Peltier Barrett, photographed in Shawnee, Oklahoma, in the 1940s. Courtesy Citizen Potawatomi Nation Cultural Center

sounds when I was afraid. She taught me to sew, knit, and embroider; she made all of the clothes for herself and her family. Gentle and strong, she bore twelve children at home and lovingly reared nine to adulthood while the men struggled in barren fields during the Dust Bowl.

My Mother, Annetta, was a gorgeous woman (and I was her 18th birthday gift). She could make anything grow and had the voice of an angel. She and her four sisters, my beautiful Aunties, guided me as I grew. What one did not know, the other could always answer, no matter how many questions I asked. Mom handled a mule and plow with the best of them. Everything that I know today, I owe to them. My childhood kitchens were the warm and happy gathering places that I remember with much joy. But no doubt, those were hard times too.

Grandma's tiny house was insulated with flour paste and newspaper. When there was enough money, she'd put up pretty flowered wallpaper. She rolled and baked feather-light biscuits and delicate, flaky, perfectly crimped pie crust. She taught me to crack eggs and mix cornmeal for the cornbread that we'd bake in a skillet seasoned with the bacon fat she kept in the red Folgers can by the stove. I'd stand on a chair turned backward to reach her counter, the apron she'd made for me out of a flour sack tied snugly around my waist.

Our powwows were held during the last week in June. It was always so, so hot and humid down in the pecan grove where the dances were held—you could barely breathe. Sometimes, a sudden thunderstorm brought a temporary

Citizen Potawatomi Nation dancers in regalia, powwow, Shawnee, Oklahoma, 1970. Author collection.

halt to the festivities, but it never seemed to cool things down—just make it more humid.

As a kid, I'd go with Grandma, Mom, and Grandpa to "the Agency" to pick up the "food products" from our reservation's Food Distribution. These commodities, "the commods"—white flour, powdered milk, lard, bricks of orange cheese product, pinto beans, and Spam—were our pantry staples. As I stood in line, I could hear women gossip and share recipes for plum jam, cornbread, corn dumplings, hominy stew, and the latest hamburger and macaroni casserole. The men stood under the shade trees, smoking their hand-rolled cigarettes and talking. At the time, I was too young to realize that I was hearing so many different Native languages. My Grandma, Mom, and Aunts spoke our native tongue—Potawatomi—but they never spoke it in front of the kids for fear we'd become "too Indian." We spoke only English in our home; yet the languages of gardening, cooking, hospitality, and generosity are encoded in my bones.

(*Left*) Loretta, age two, wearing a Japanese outfit her Father brought back from World War II. Author collection.
(*Right*) Loretta's sons, Clayton Barrett Oden and Craig Lamar Oden, ages 4 and 2. Author collection.

I grew up in two very different worlds divided by class and culture. My Mom's Potawatomie family lived apart from my Dad's family, whose ancestors had crossed on the *Mayflower*. (My Dad's Mom, Grandma Deenie, was a card-carrying member of the DAR, Daughters of the American Revolution.)

Dad taught me to ride horseback and to hunt. We'd head out to the duck blind on cold, misty mornings, sip black coffee, and use his specially carved duck calls. Surprisingly, my very genteel Grandma Deenie was an avid fisherwoman. She and I would fish until late in the evening; she was quite adept at gutting, scaling, and frying our catch in a pan.

Our two families did not mingle, so as I grew, I learned to walk in two worlds and be as independent and fearless as the women who raised me. My very happiest years were spent raising two sons, Clay and Craig, on our beautiful ranch land just north of Oklahoma City, not far from both of my families' homes. Growing up, our boys helped with the cattle, horses, a pet pig, cats, dogs, and rabbits. We planted a huge garden and harvested plums, apples, and pears from the orchard. Our sons were good hunters too, and they learned to dress the duck, quail, pheasant, and occasional squirrel they bagged. When they left for college, and my nest was empty, I knew then it was time to spread my wings.

At age 48, I yearned to learn about this world. I needed to travel, to grow, to research my ancestral lineage to understand myself and my life's purpose. I moved to LA to start fresh, and it was there, as I began to meet other members of my extended Potawatomi family and explore my heritage, that a lightbulb went off in my head. I could get Italian food, French food, this food, that food, from chefs who could trace their culinary roots. But what, I wanted to know, did my ancestors eat? It couldn't have been fry bread and Indian tacos. So I reached out to my relations in other regions—elders, wise men and women—and began tracking down traditional cooks who practiced the "old ways." Just about every person I met sent me off to meet another cook or elder they thought I should talk to. Then that person would send me off to someone else.

As I traveled among the Northern Woodlands and the Great Lakes, I harvested wild rice in canoes and tapped maple trees and boiled sap into syrup and sugar. Along the East Coast, I cooked lobsters, crabs, and fish on the beaches and learned to make authentic Iroquois white cornbread. All through the Gulf Coast's bayous and marshlands, I cooked crawfish and alligator with the elders and learned gumbo from the Houma, the Chitamacha, and the Choctaw. I witnessed firsthand how our mountains, rivers, lakes, and oceans have defined how we live, and I came to understand that our Native cuisine is as rich and varied as that of France, Italy, or any other country.

I knew, of course, the hard, devastating history of Native Americans, of the impact of colonization on our traditions, language, culture, and health, especially our health. Before European contact, diabetes, obesity, heart disease, and tooth decay—all chronic health issues linked to diet—did not exist in our tribes. Today, because of the Native American diet based on commodity foods, many of our people are suffering terribly: among the Tohono O'odham (Pima) of southern Arizona, to take but one example, 70 percent of the population has diabetes. Oklahoma itself is the fourth most obese state in the country.

As Dr. John Mohawk, the revered Seneca scholar whom I met on my journey, has said, our health, our environment, our climate, and our future depend on maintaining an intimate relationship with the natural world. I saw my purpose as working with food to forge those connections and thus heal our bodies, nature, and communities.

Thanks to my Grandmothers, Mom, and Aunties, I knew how to cook. And I'd had some restaurant experience working in the oldest barbecue joint in Oklahoma, Van's Pig Stand, owned by my first husband's family. After crisscrossing the continent from the shores of the Pacific Northwest to the southeast tip of Florida—visiting reservations, cooking with the elders, diligently recording recipes—it was time for me to act. As far as I knew, very few restaurants served tribal specialties—Puget Sound oysters, Shawnee wild elk, Navajo squash soup, Minnesota wild rice, and Houma shrimp.

In 1993, my son Clay and I opened Corn Dance Café, the first restaurant to truly showcase the vast variety and diversity of Indigenous foods of the Americas. We chose Santa Fe for its bounty of local ingredients and took over Maria Ysabelle's New Mexican Food at the end of a dead-end street. We rolled up our sleeves and got to work, fixing the rotted floor, replacing antiquated equipment, and sanding and painting rickety chairs and old tables in brilliant crayon colors. We engaged local craftspeople and artists who traded their time and talent for our dishes—a metalsmith created a gorgeous iron gate for the courtyard, and local photographers, weavers, and painters hung their art on our

FRY BREAD SOAPBOX

Perhaps the biggest misunderstanding around Native food relates to fry bread. While it's considered a "traditional Native American dish," I don't remember eating fry bread when I was a kid. My Mom never made fry bread, nor did my Grandma or any of my Aunts. (We ate our share of biscuits and gravy, though!) What I do know is that the origin of fry bread lies in the history of our people. The removal of tribes from their homelands led to the government commodity program that provided white flour and lard, the key fry bread ingredients. People were poor and hungry: white-flour dough fried in lard tastes good and can fill you up. The years went by, and fry bread spread, mostly through the powwow circuit, until it became iconic. But fry bread has wreaked havoc on the health of Native people.

Loretta's Cornmeal Fry Bread (page 165)
Little Big Pies (page 167)

(*Left*) The second Corn Dance Café, inside the Hotel Santa Fe, 1990s. Author collection.
(*Right*) With the two male leads in the movie *Smoke Signals* (1998), Adam Beach (*left*) and
Evan Adams, at Corn Dance Café. Author collection.

walls. Our quirky, casual Southwestern vibe drew members of AIM (American
Indian Movement), along with a roster of celebrities—Graham Greene, Joy
Harjo, Buffy Sainte-Marie, Sherman Alexie, N. Scott Momaday, Ali McGraw,
Wes Studi, Gene Hackman, and Marsha Mason, to name just a few. They loved
the food, and I was able to protect them from their curious fans. We received
great reviews and opened a second Corn Dance Café in the Hotel Santa Fe,
owned by Picuris Pueblo. Both locations featured courtyard tipis.

Our dishes of pre–European contact ingredients—bison, rabbit, elk, wild
rice, quinoa, and the Three Sisters (corn, beans, and squash)—combined classic
culinary, home cooking, and ancient practices, such as smoking and salting.
Our menu reflected dishes from Nunavut to Tierra del Fuego.

We made sure that the atmosphere at Corn Dance Café was calm and
peaceful. I was adamant that my kitchen would be a safe place where everyone
would be treated with respect! The atmosphere was encouraging. No yelling
or throwing dishes. No tantrums. On weekends, a Native artist played his
hand-carved flutes.

The theme that was established at Corn Dance, and that I hope resonates
through all my work, is that food is sacred. When I cook and present at confer-
ences or am simply serving those who now dine at Thirty Nine Restaurant
at First Americans Museum, I am intent that this beautiful, healing food be
prepared, served, and enjoyed with respect.

Corn Dance Café drew national attention in travel magazines and on
the food pages of major newspapers. I was invited to cook on *Good Morning
America*, *Today*, and the Food Network, and these appearances were always
scheduled at Thanksgiving. Thanksgiving morning on *Good Morning America*,

In the kitchen with Dustin Bagnaro in US Foods Test Kitchen for the FAM Museum tasting, November 2018, Oklahoma City.

Thanksgiving morning on *Today*. It was just insane! Anytime the media wanted an Indian, they called me. I realized that we were considered an extinct species, though we are everywhere. I seized these media opportunities to share our history and culture through food and created the TV series I hosted for PBS—*Seasoned with Spirit*. It earned an Emmy award.

I moved back to Oklahoma because I had grandkids sprouting up. Clay died, suddenly and devastatingly, and my life has never been the same. I took the heartbreak and focused on healing myself, and our people. Food is medicine! Healthy, natural food is a powerful tool in addressing the issues related to the American diet. So for the past thirty years, I've served as a mentor, teacher, and food justice advocate, sharing my knowledge and passion.

I've helped forge an intertribal network of ranchers, farmers, and fishermen, creating jobs as well as nurturing young people. Nothing gives me more pleasure than sharing my experiences with cooks of all ages—from working with our Native kids in summer gardening and cooking programs to working with elders on health issues. I've created programs and classes for college students, community leaders, nutritionists, and health professionals.

I'm a founding council member of the Native American Food Sovereignty Alliance, working shoulder to shoulder, spatula to spatula, to connect tribal citizens across the country to our traditional growing and cooking practices. I have had to navigate the complicated politics of this region, indeed our country, to try to create culturally relevant dishes to make our people proud.

My work is more than just creating dishes and talking about them. I believe we are connected to life when we sit down together over a good meal. In our fast-paced, tech-saturated, attention-deficit-disordered culture, we must recover the art of dining. Psychologists posit that each of us has one or two primary means by which we communicate (and receive) love, but they don't typically include food as a love language. Nothing brings me more pleasure than preparing a meal for others. Doing so is my expression of caring and respect. It is also a great responsibility. I use food as the forum to speak to my own community, the broader Native community, and to non-Native people. If we can come together at the table, we will come together in peace.

Loretta in Santa Fe, spreading dough for a Little Big Pie. Photo by Kitty Leaken.

For as long as I can, I will cook for events and educate the next generation. My most recent endeavor is as the Indigenous food consultant to Thirty Nine Restaurant at First Americans Museum in Oklahoma City. This is how I share my knowledge, and this is what truly sustains me. Even when I am exhausted from traveling, presenting, and cooking, I'm satisfied knowing that I've inspired younger Native chefs, farmers, producers, educators, policy makers, health professionals, home cooks, and eaters.

For me, the kitchen is a special space of cultural geography that connects me back to my female relatives and ancestors who nurtured each successive generation to make my presence here possible. The kitchen is where I pay this legacy forward to the current and future generations across Turtle Island and beyond. As a woman chef, I'm so proud of our rising Native female chefs. It's a tough profession that requires stamina, commitment, and often courage to change the way we all think about food.

My intention in writing this book is to share our rich food traditions with all people. I've lectured and cooked for broad audiences—the Institute of American

Discussing sunchokes and summer squash at Slow Food USA, Denver, 2017. Author collection.

Indian Arts, Slow Food, the Heard and Autry museums; I have been instrumental in creating the Turtle Island convivium of Slow Food; and I have presented to gatherings in Tokyo, Canada, and Italy and throughout the United States. What thrills me most? The many young and talented Indigenous chefs bringing this work into the future. They are creating menus of healthy dishes—plant forward, seasonal, regional, gluten free, dairy free, low glycemic—beautiful, delicious meals that promise to heal the Earth and us as well.

The recipes you'll find in this book are focused on flavor, our sense of place, and how the meals I serve come together. You'll find snacks and small plates, soups and salads, plant-powered main dishes, free-range and wild meat and poultry, and, of course, desserts. (I'm mad about chocolate.) Here, too, are refreshing teas and spirited drinks, plus condiments, sauces, and salsas to have on hand. Many of these recipes are inspired by the bold, rich flavors I came to love in Santa Fe—the chiles, wood-roasted game, and vibrant salads. I often blend regional specialties to create a balanced dish: some represent the bounty of Turtle Island—Native foods that I grew up with and discovered across Indian Country; others represent pantry staples of our Oklahoma cuisine—wheat flour, sugar, dairy, and ranch meats. You'll find sources for my favorite ingredients listed at the end of this book. The recipes you'll find here are created with respect and gratitude for all our relations. So please, let's cook together and come to the table. Migwech! Let's eat!

(*Left*) The Three Sisters growing in the backyard of Loretta's Oklahoma City home: heirloom butternut squash, red corn, and beans. Author collection.

(*Right*) In the dining room at Thirty Nine Restaurant, First Americans Museum, Oklahoma City, 2022. Photo courtesy OKC Edible/Corrigan Tyrell.

Big Little Plates

Spicy Sage Popcorn 17

White Bean Hummus 18

Easy Tomatillo Guacamole 21

Thirty Nine Restaurant
Roasted Corn Ribs 22

Sweet Potato Griddle Cakes 25

Three Sisters Sauté with Sage Pesto 28

Corn Blini with Caviar 30

When Clay and I opened Corn Dance Café, we did not know much about running a restaurant, but we knew how to cook and make guests feel welcome. These whimsical light bites say, "Come on in, ya'll, and sit a while." Several are hearty enough to serve as a light meal, especially when paired with any of the soups or salads in the chapter "Beautiful Bowls."

Spicy Sage Popcorn

Soon after we opened Corn Dance Café, a friend from Picuris Pueblo stopped by with a jar of his home-fried, salted cicadas. "These will make great bar snacks," he said. "Salty, makes people real thirsty." We opted to make fresh popcorn well seasoned with cayenne and sage instead. This popcorn was the favorite bar snack at Corn Dance Café. It also makes a fragrant garnish for soup.

Serves 12 (makes about 14 cups)

1 cup fresh sage leaves

2 tablespoons vegetable oil

½ cup popcorn kernels

1 tablespoon good-quality extra-virgin olive oil

1 teaspoon poultry seasoning (see note)

Generous pinch of cayenne

Coarse salt

Lay the sage on a plate in one layer, and microwave until it's crisp, about 2½ minutes. Remove, crumble the sage into a dish, and set it aside.

Put the vegetable oil into a large pot set over medium-high heat, and add the popcorn. Cover, and shake until the kernels pop, about 8 to 10 minutes. Turn the popcorn into a paper bag, drizzle it with the olive oil, and shake to coat. Add the crumbled sage, poultry seasoning, cayenne, and salt to taste, and shake again before serving.

Note: You can find poultry seasoning in the spice aisle of your grocery store, but it's easy enough to make your own. It will keep for about 9 months in a covered jar and is great to keep on hand for seasoning poultry as well as popcorn. Simply grind these ingredients together in a spice grinder or with a mortar and pestle: 2 teaspoons sage, 1½ teaspoons thyme, 1 teaspoon marjoram, and 1 teaspoon rosemary.

White Bean Hummus

This hummus is brighter and fresher tasting than most hummus made with chickpeas because it's made without tahini. It calls for cooked tepary beans, which have a lovely, rich earthy flavor. But if you're in a rush, feel free to use canned cannellini beans. Vary the recipe by adding a little roasted sweet potatoes or squash for color and flavor. Serve the hummus with jicama sticks and tortilla chips.

Makes about 2 generous cups

¼ cup extra-virgin olive oil, plus more as needed

3 cloves garlic, coarsely chopped

1½ dried tepary beans, soaked overnight and cooked (see Tepary Beans, page 19), or 4 cups canned cannellini beans, rinsed and drained

¼ cup lemon juice

1 teaspoon ground cumin

2 teaspoons finely chopped parsley

Salt

½ teaspoon Coleman's Dry Mustard

Pinch cayenne (optional)

Put all of the ingredients into a food processor fitted with a steel blade, and pulse until the beans have reached the desired consistency. You may add a little more olive oil to make it creamier. Taste, and adjust the seasonings. Store the hummus in a covered container in the refrigerator for up to a week.

Sweet potato or pumpkin variation: Pulse ¼ cup of cooked sweet potato or pumpkin into the hummus, and amp up the flavor with a hit of chile pepper and a squirt of lime juice.

TEPARY BEANS

These ancient beans are a superfood of the Sonoran Desert. White tepary beans are noted for their unique and delicious naturally sweet flavor and creamy texture. The brown variety are more savory and slightly nutty. Cultivated for at least a thousand years by the Natives of the Sonoran Desert—the Akimel O'odham and the Tohono O'odham, who continue to grow them on their reservation lands with summer rainfall in arroyos and limited irrigation along the Gila River—the tepary bean is believed to be the world's most drought-tolerant bean. It is higher in fiber and protein than most other beans, with a low glycemic index and a unique taste.

Tepary beans are tougher than other dried beans, so they take longer to cook. To cook them, put the beans in a pot and add enough water to cover by 4 inches. Soak the beans overnight. Drain the beans, and add enough water to cover the beans by 4 inches. Set the pot over high heat, and bring the water to a boil. Reduce the heat, cover, and simmer until the beans are tender, about 1 to 1½ hours, adding more water as needed.

Easy Tomatillo Guacamole

Set out this guacamole with corn chips and jicama sticks, or serve it with cornbread as a side to Clay's Buffaloaf (page 136).

Makes about 2½ cups

½ pound tomatillos, husks removed

1 jalapeño

3 avocados, peeled, pitted, and coarsely chopped

½ cup chopped cilantro

1 tablespoon fresh lime juice, or more to taste

½ salt, or to taste

On a hot grill or under a broiler, char the tomatillos and the jalapeño. Using a damp paper towel, rub any of the charred peel off the jalapeño, and remove the seeds. Chop the jalapeño and the tomatillos, and transfer them to a medium bowl.

Add the avocados to the bowl. With the back of a fork, mash the avocado with the tomatillos and jalapeño, and then mash in the lime juice and salt. Taste, and adjust the seasonings.

Thirty Nine Restaurant Roasted Corn Ribs

These "ribs" are the most popular appetizer on Thirty Nine's menu. When cut into quarters and roasted, they curl a bit and become golden and caramel sweet—perfect hand-held nibbles. This recipe is the result of a simple experiment. We had been offering roasted corn wheels, but on a whim tried cutting the ears into ribs instead and discovered that they curled in the heat. The corn ribs make a pretty impression on the plate.

Serves 4

4 ears of corn, shucked

Extra-virgin olive oil

Cilantro oil (see note on page 65)

¼ cup crumbled Cotija cheese (optional)

Coarse salt

Preheat the oven to 400 degrees. Quarter the corn lengthwise. Drizzle the corn with the olive oil, and place it on a baking sheet. Roast the corn until the kernels begin to turn golden, turning the corn occasionally, about 10 to 15 minutes. Keep an eye on the corn, and remove it as soon as it begins to curl: it turns tough and chewy if overcooked. Remove the corn from the oven, and serve it drizzled with cilantro oil and sprinkled with the cheese (if using). Season with salt to taste.

Sweet Potato Griddle Cakes

This recipe is the creation of Chef Caesaré Assad, a bright star in my world. We were cooking for an event at Full Belly Farm in California and had spent the day foraging ingredients. The farm had built us a roaring fire of almond wood for grilling. Caesaré tossed a few of the sweet potatoes into the coals to roast. Once they were tender, she created these beautiful patties, topped each with a tiny quail egg, and grilled them over the fire. She then garnished them with amaranth sprouts and cilantro sprouts. They make a lovely appetizer.

Serves 4 to 6

2 large sweet potatoes, about ¼ pound each

1 tablespoon extra-virgin olive oil

1 jalapeño, seeded and finely chopped

1 medium shallot, minced

Salt

1 large egg

¼ cup corn or wheat flour for dusting

2 to 4 tablespoons vegetable oil, more as needed

4 to 6 quail eggs or small chicken eggs

Amaranth sprouts and cilantro sprouts, or micro greens, for garnish

Preheat the oven to 350 degrees. Score a large X in the center of each sweet potato, and place them on a baking sheet. Bake until tender, about 45 to 50 minutes. Remove, and allow to cool enough to handle. Peel the sweet potatoes, and transfer the flesh into a medium bowl.

Heat the olive oil in a small skillet, and lightly sauté the jalapeño and the shallot until fragrant. Transfer them to the bowl with the sweet potatoes, mash them together, and season to taste with salt. Mash in the egg to make a soft dough. Shape the dough into patties. (Use about ½ cup of dough per patty if topping with chicken eggs; use about ⅓ cup of dough per patty if topping with quail eggs.)

Reduce the oven temperature to 300 degrees. Line a baking sheet with parchment paper.

Film a large skillet with the vegetable oil, and set it over medium heat. Dredge the patties in corn flour, place them in the skillet, and lightly pan-fry for about 2 to 4 minutes per side. Transfer the patties to a baking sheet, and make an impression in each one. Crack an egg into each impression. Bake until the eggs are set, about 4 to 6 minutes for the quail eggs or about 15 to 20 minutes for the chicken eggs. Serve garnished with the amaranth and cilantro sprouts.

THE THREE SISTERS

Many Indigenous people plant corn, beans, and squash—known as the Three Sisters—together. According to Potawatomi legend, Three Sisters were to set out to different hunting grounds. Because they did not want to be separated, they went to play in the moonlight one last time. In the morning, when their parents went to find the girls, corn, squash, and beans grew in their place. It's told that the older, tallest sister is the corn stalk, the baby sister is the bean, and the shorter, rounder little sister is the squash. The corn stalk provides a pole for the bean to climb. The bean fixes the nitrogen in the soil that the corn depletes. The squash leaves shelter the roots of the corn and bean from the sun and help retain water while smothering out pesky weeds. Even though Native people have been growing food this way for eons, it's known today as companion planting, a process that is fundamental to permaculture growing practices.

Three Sisters Sauté with Sage Pesto

This colorful dish makes a lovely starter, a fine side dish, and a light meal when paired with cornbread. I think of it as a warm salad.

Serves 4 to 6

½ cup dried heirloom beans, soaked overnight and cooked (see note), or 1 (15-ounce) can beans

1 pound mixed baby squashes (such as pattypan, sunburst, and zucchini) or mature zucchini or yellow squash, unpeeled

3 tablespoons extra-virgin olive oil, or to taste

2 cups sweet corn kernels, fresh or frozen

1 cup chopped ripe Roma tomatoes

Salt

⅓ cup Sage Pesto (page 225)

If using larger zucchini, cut the squashes into very thin ribbons using a mandolin, spiralizer, or sharp knife, or dice the squash into bite-sized pieces.

Heat the oil in a large skillet, and sauté the squash for about 1 minute. Stirring after each addition, toss in the beans, corn, tomatoes, and then a dollop of sage pesto. Season with salt. Serve immediately, before the vegetables go limp.

Note: Put the beans into a large dish, and add enough water to cover by 4 inches. Soak overnight. Drain the beans, and transfer them to a large saucepan. Add enough water to cover the beans by 4 inches. Set the saucepan over high heat, and bring the water to a boil. Reduce the heat, and simmer the beans, covered, until they're tender, about 35 to 45 minutes (older beans may need longer). Drain the beans.

Corn Blini with Caviar

Trout roe, paddlefish roe, salmon roe, sturgeon roe. All fish lay eggs, and all fish eggs make wonderful caviar. On a PBS film shoot, we went up the Klamath River in Northern California to a Yurok village. Our host brought out a large egg pouch from a freshly caught sturgeon and, after cleaning it, presented us with about ten pounds of roe, or caviar. She lined a baking pan with fresh maple leaves and put the roe into the pan to roast over an open fire. It cooked into a flat bread that she cut into squares. It was so unbelievably rich, the briny eggs roasted with sweet and smoky maple leaves. Pure decadence on the river's edge.

We can't replicate the caviar bread ($$$), but this corn blini will serve us well.

Serves 4 to 6

¼ cup all-purpose flour

¾ cup cornmeal

½ teaspoon baking powder

1 teaspoon salt

¾ cup milk

1 large egg

2 to 3 tablespoons vegetable oil

4 to 6 tablespoons caviar

Avocado cream (see note)

In a large bowl, stir together both flours, baking powder, and salt. In a separate bowl, whisk together the milk and the egg, and then whisk it into the flour mixture.

Heat 1 tablespoon of the oil in a medium sauté pan over medium heat. With a tablespoon, portion out the batter into the pan, being careful not to overcrowd. Cook until bubbles form on the top side of the blini, about 2 minutes. Flip the blini, and cook for 2 more minutes, or until browned. Repeat with the remaining batter. Clean the hot pan with a dry paper towel between batches.

Serve the blini with a dollop of caviar topped with a little avocado cream.

Note: To make avocado cream, blend ¼ cup diced avocado with 2 tablespoons sour cream or Greek yogurt, 2 teaspoons lime juice, and salt to taste.

POKE

Poke, a beloved sign of spring, is one of those foods I grew up with, but you won't find it on menus, in grocery stores, or at farmers markets. It's an emblem of our thriftiness and resilience, and it's prized for its antiviral properties, believed to heal a variety of infections and inflammatory conditions. This towering perennial weed with oblong leaves and magenta berries and stalks is delicious; yet, it can be toxic if not properly handled. It must be harvested early in the spring, when the plant is young with tender green leaves, before it bolts. It must first be boiled and rinsed at least two times before eating.

The boiled green has an asparagus-spinach flavor and is usually sautéed in bacon grease with onions and eggs, then served topped with crumbled cooked bacon. The dish is called poke sallet—*sallet* being the French term for a "mess of greens cooked until tender." (That's my definition, and I'm sticking to it!)

Beautiful Bowls

SALADS AND SOUPS

Three Sisters and Friends Salad 36

Pineapple, Jicama, and Avocado Salad 40

Tomato and Corn Salad with
Balsamic Vinaigrette 41

Nopales and Fiery Mango Salad
with Chipotle Vinaigrette 42

Jicama Slaw 45

Ribbons of Butternut Squash and Baby
Rocket with Cranberry Vinaigrette
and Sunflower Seeds 49

The Old Aldridge Hotel Iceberg
Wedge with Sweet Corn Vinaigrette
and Tomato-Sumac Dressing 50

Sunchoke, Jicama, Avocado, and Pineapple
Salad with Spicy Vinaigrette 51

Mom's Classic Yellow Potato Salad 54

These salads and soups are vegetable-centered, using what's fresh from the garden through the season. Grandma Peltier was an avid gardener. She taught me to plant the Three Sisters—corn, beans, and squash—showing me how to draw a circle in the garden dirt, create a mound in the center, and form a moat to capture the water and compost. We ringed the garden with marigolds to draw out the aphids. Later, when Mom, Clay, Craig, and I gardened, we had learned to add earthworms to aerate the soil and ladybugs to defeat the predators.

Three Sisters and Friends Salad

This is my iconic dish! I have been making it since the earliest days of Corn Dance Café. It's what I serve close friends, and it's what I make ahead for big feasts. The ingredients vary slightly depending on the season and whatever I happen to have on hand. If you're in a pinch, by all means, substitute canned ingredients for those cooked from scratch. It will hold at least a day in a covered container in the refrigerator.

Serves 4 to 6

VINAIGRETTE

1 clove garlic, minced

¼ teaspoon red pepper flakes

¼ teaspoon ground coriander

⅛ teaspoon sea salt

½ cup extra-virgin olive oil

¼ cup seasoned rice vinegar

1 teaspoon fresh lime juice

SALAD

½ cup dried heirloom beans, soaked overnight, or 1 (15-ounce) can black beans, drained and rinsed

½ cup quinoa (a mix of red, black, and white or all one color)

½ cup hand-harvested wild rice

½ cup lightly grilled or roasted corn kernels (see note)

½ cup diced tender, small zucchini or summer squash, unpeeled

½ cup cherry tomatoes, halved

3 tablespoons chopped cilantro

1 tablespoon minced red onion

1 clove garlic, minced

½ teaspoon serrano chile, seeded, deveined, and minced

¼ teaspoon sea salt

Vinaigrette: In a small bowl, whisk together the ingredients for the vinaigrette.

Salad: Drain the beans, and transfer them to a large saucepan. Add enough water to cover the beans by 4 inches. Set the saucepan over high heat, and bring the water to a boil. Reduce the heat, and simmer the beans, covered, until they're tender, about 35 to 45 minutes (older beans may need to cook longer). Drain the beans.

Rinse the quinoa thoroughly. Bring 2 cups of water to a boil, and add the quinoa. Reduce the heat, cover, and simmer on medium-low until the quinoa's germ, or tail, appears, about 12 to 15 minutes. Remove the pot from the heat, drain any remaining water from the quinoa, and fluff it with a fork.

Rinse the wild rice under cold running water until it runs clear. Transfer it to a pot, and add enough water to cover the rice by 4 inches. Set the pot over high heat, and bring the water to a boil. Reduce the heat, and simmer until the rice opens and is tender, about 20 to 25 minutes. Drain off any excess water.

In a large bowl, toss together the beans, quinoa, wild rice, corn, zucchini, tomatoes, cilantro, onion, garlic, chile, and salt. Drizzle half of the vinaigrette over the salad ingredients, and toss to coat. Taste, and add more vinaigrette as needed. Store any extra vinaigrette in a covered container in the refrigerator for up to 2 weeks.

Note: To roast corn kernels, film a skillet with a little oil, and set it over medium-high heat. Add the corn kernels, and sauté until they're nicely browned, about 5 to 10 minutes. Remove and cool before adding the roasted corn to the batter. You can also grill a whole ear of corn over an open fire until it's lightly toasted. Remove the corn and, when cool, cut the kernels from the cob.

WILD RICE

Hand-harvested wild rice comes from the cold waters near the Great Lakes. It is harvested using long poles (called knockers) that gently knock the seeds into the boat. From there, it's spread out to dry on tarps where red-winged blackbirds feast on the rice worms. It's then toasted in kettles and threshed. This wild rice is quite different from the cultivated rice grown in paddies. It cooks quickly.

To cook real wild rice, rinse the rice under cold running water until it runs clear. Transfer it to a pot, and add enough water to cover the rice by 4 inches. Set the pot over high heat, and bring the water to a boil. Reduce the heat, and simmer until the rice opens and is tender, about 20 to 25 minutes. Watch, and be careful not to overcook the rice. Drain off any excess water from the pot before serving.

Pineapple, Jicama, and Avocado Salad

Crunchy jicama and creamy avocado team up in this festive salad. The fresh pineapple makes a fine, sweet touch. It's great on the holiday table.

Serves 4 to 6

1 serrano chile, seeded
and minced

½ cup minced cilantro

2 tablespoons fresh lime juice

2 tablespoon seasoned
rice vinegar

¼ cup extra-virgin olive oil

½ teaspoon coarse salt

2 cups cubed fresh pineapple

1 medium jicama, peeled
and cut into matchsticks

3 cups red leaf lettuce,
arugula, or frisée

1 avocado, peeled, pitted,
and cubed

In a medium bowl, whisk together the chile, cilantro, lime juice, vinegar, oil, and salt. Add the pineapple chunks and jicama sticks, and let them marinate for about 30 minutes.

Arrange the lettuce on chilled salad plates or a large platter. Remove the jicama and pineapple from the marinade, arrange them over the lettuce, and then top with the avocado. Drizzle a little of the vinaigrette over the salad right before serving.

Tomato and Corn Salad with Balsamic Vinaigrette

I often add thinly sliced Vidalia or Maui onions to this bright, summery salad.

Serves 4 to 6

6 ears sweet corn, husked

5 tablespoons extra-virgin olive oil

1 tablespoon fresh garlic, minced

½ cup packed fresh basil leaves, julienned

5 plum tomatoes, seeded and chopped

1 cup cubed jicama

3 tablespoons balsamic vinegar

Salt

Pepper flakes

Using a large knife, cut the kernels from the cob (and save the cobs for the stockpot). Heat 2 tablespoons of the oil in a heavy skillet set over medium heat. Add the garlic and the corn and sauté for about 2 minutes. Remove the pan from the heat, and toss in half of the basil leaves. Put the corn mixture into a bowl, and let it cool slightly. Toss in the tomatoes, jicama, vinegar, remaining oil, and remaining basil leaves. Season with salt and red pepper flakes to taste. Serve warm or at room temperature.

Nopales and Fiery Mango Salad with Chipotle Vinaigrette

This recipe calls for nopales (aka nopalitos), the flat paddles of the prickly pear cactus. Here, they're paired with tangy-sweet pineapple and red bell peppers and topped with crunchy pumpkin seeds. This dressing is also delicious drizzled over grilled chicken or roasted fish.

Serves 4

VINAIGRETTE

- 1 mango, peeled and pitted, or 1 cup frozen, thawed mango
- Juice of 1 medium orange, about ½ cup
- 1 tablespoon fresh lime juice
- ½ to 1 teaspoon dried chipotle flakes
- ½ teaspoon chopped fresh rosemary
- ¼ cup extra-virgin olive oil

SALAD

- 12 nopales, trimmed, blanched, and cut into 3-inch strips (see Nopales, page 43)
- 1 red bell pepper, seeded and cut into ¼-inch strips
- 1 cup pineapple chunks
- 1 cup toasted pumpkin seeds (see note on page 65)

Vinaigrette: In a blender or a food processor fitted with a steel blade, puree the vinaigrette ingredients together until very smooth. Store any leftover vinaigrette in a covered container in the refrigerator.

Salad: Put the nopales, bell pepper, and pineapple into a bowl, and toss them with enough of the dressing to lightly coat. Serve sprinkled with toasted pumpkin seeds.

NOPALES

Nopales, or cactus paddles, can be daunting at first, but are truly worth the effort. Their flavor is slightly tart, and they are crunchy with a soft, sticky flesh that resembles okra. Look for paddles that are bright green and not limp. Be careful cleaning nopales; given their prickles, you may want to wear heavy rubber gloves. Rinse the paddles under cold water, being careful with the thorns. Using a vegetable peeler or a sharp knife, peel away the bumps and thorns. Lay the paddle on a chopping board, and trim off about ¼ inch of the edges and about ½ inch of the base. They're good grilled or sautéed.

To prepare nopales for salads, blanch them in a pot of rapidly boiling water for about 2 to 3 minutes. Then turn them into a strainer, and refresh them under cold running water to stop the cooking and rinse off the sliminess.

Jicama Slaw

Crunchy, tart, and creamy, this simple slaw is a perfect side to the Spicy Houma Shrimp (page 105) or Best Fried Fish (page 94).

Serves 4

DRESSING

- 1 tablespoon extra-virgin olive oil
- 1 clove garlic, minced
- ½ small ripe avocado
- 1 tablespoon chopped cilantro
- 1 teaspoon lime zest
- 2 tablespoons lime juice
- 1 teaspoon honey
- ½ teaspoon chipotle powder
  Generous pinch salt

SLAW

- 1 pound jicama, peeled and cut into matchstick-sized pieces
- 2 tablespoons chopped cilantro
- 1 tablespoon salted, roasted squash seeds

Dressing: In a blender or a food processor fitted with a steel blade, buzz together the oil, garlic, avocado, 1 tablespoon of cilantro, lime zest and juice, honey, and chipotle powder. Add salt to taste. If the mixture seems too thick, buzz in a tablespoon or two or water.

Slaw: Put the jicama into a medium bowl, and toss it with just enough dressing to lightly coat. Sprinkle with 2 tablespoons of cilantro and the squash seeds.

NOTES FROM LORETTA'S KITCHEN

~~~~~~~~~~~~~~~~~~~~~~~~

WATERCRESS

Wild watercress grows along fast-running streams in the early spring, often before the crusty snow along the banks has melted. It's distinctly peppery with a clean, bright taste. If you harvest wild watercress, be sure to return any snails that cling to the leaves back to the stream. They will do more for the quality of the water than humans ever can.

~~~~~~~~~~~~~~~~~~~~~~~~

Ribbons of Butternut Squash and Baby Rocket with Cranberry Vinaigrette and Sunflower Seeds

Pretty ribbons of raw butternut squash make for a light, crisp autumn salad. Here, they're marinated in a sharp cranberry vinaigrette. Look for a small, fresh butternut squash with a long neck; it's much easier to shave. You will end up with more vinaigrette than you need for this salad. Store it in a covered jar in the refrigerator, and use it to marinate poultry, fish, and seafood.

Serves 4 to 6

VINAIGRETTE

- ¼ cup rice wine vinegar
- ½ teaspoon minced garlic
- ½ tablespoon fresh lemon juice
- ¼ cup minced cilantro
- 2 tablespoons wildflower honey, or to taste
- ½ teaspoon Dijon mustard
- 1 teaspoon ground coriander
- 1 tablespoon finely minced unsweetened dried cranberries
- ¾ cup extra-virgin olive oil
- Pinch of sea salt

SALAD

- 1 butternut squash, halved, seeded, and peeled
- 2 cups watercress, spinach, or other dark green, stemmed
- 2 cups baby rocket (arugula)
- ¼ cup toasted sunflower seeds
- Unsweetened dried cranberries, for garnish
- Toasted sunflower seeds, for garnish

Vinaigrette: Put all the ingredients except the oil into a blender or a food processor fitted with a steel blade, and whir until pureed. With the motor running, add the oil in a slow, steady stream.

Salad: Using a vegetable peeler or a very thin knife, cut the squash lengthwise into long ribbons. In a large bowl, toss together the ribbons of squash, watercress, and rocket.

Drizzle in just enough vinaigrette to lightly coat the salad ingredients and toss. Serve garnished with dried cranberries and sunflower seeds.

The Old Aldridge Hotel Iceberg Wedge with Sweet Corn Vinaigrette and Tomato-Sumac Dressing

Going out for dinner was a big event in our family, and going to the Aldridge Hotel's steak house restaurant was *the* big event. I loved getting all dressed up and was expected to sit "like a lady." Wow! I felt so grown-up. My grandparents (on my Dad's side) always ordered the "house" salad—a big wedge of iceberg lettuce with not one but two dressings! My early memories of that salad inspired this rendition crowned with a creamy sweet corn vinaigrette and tangy sumac dressing—think Kraft Italian and Russian bottled dressings of the day, but our version is all local, all good!

You can purchase sumac at most Middle Eastern food shops or in the bulk spice section of most natural food co-ops. It also grows wild as staghorn sumac. The branches bend up and bear cone-shaped clusters of sumac berries that can be dried, sifted, and used as a spice. The small heads of lettuce are served sliced in thirds, drizzled with each of the dressings, and garnished with a bit of crumbled wasna, or gazhakdek wiyas (see Bison Jerky, page 139), or, as they did at the Aldridge, simply some crumbled bacon bits.

Do try the two different dressings on grilled meat, fish, and roasted vegetables.

Serves 4 to 6

TOMATO-SUMAC DRESSING
Makes about ¾ cup

1 teaspoon minced garlic

3 tablespoons fresh lemon juice

2 tablespoons fresh tomato juice

2 teaspoons sumac

Generous pinch salt

1 tablespoon agave syrup

6 tablespoons extra-virgin olive oil

SWEET CORN VINAIGRETTE
Makes about 1 cup

1 ear corn

¼ cup extra-virgin olive oil

¼ cup lime juice, from about 2 limes

1 tablespoon honey

¼ cup chopped fresh cilantro

Pinch salt

SALAD
4 to 6 whole heads baby iceberg lettuce or 1 large head iceberg lettuce, cut into 4 to 6 wedges

1 large tomato, cut into 1-inch dice

¼ cup chopped or shredded wasna, or crumbled cooked bacon

Tomato-Sumac Dressing: In small bowl, whisk together the garlic, lemon juice, tomato juice, sumac, salt, and agave syrup. Slowly whisk in the oil until it's fully incorporated. Store in a covered jar in the refrigerator for up to 2 weeks.

Sweet Corn Vinaigrette: Using a sharp knife, cut the corn from the cob into a bowl. Use the dull side of the knife to scrape any remaining bits of corn and corn milk into the bowl with the corn kernels. Turn half of the corn with all of the corn milk into a blender or a food processor fitted with a steel blade. Pulse to puree the corn. Pour the pureed corn into a bowl, stir in the remaining corn, and whisk in the remaining ingredients.

Salad: Arrange the lettuce on a large platter or individual plates. Sprinkle the diced tomato over the lettuce. Drizzle the lettuce with each of the dressings, and garnish it with wasna.

Sunchoke, Jicama, Avocado, and Pineapple Salad with Spicy Vinaigrette

The tangy-sweet pineapple and creamy avocado bring back memories of wonderful meals in Acapulco on my cooking adventures researching Indigenous foods through Mexico, Bolivia, and Peru. It's too easy to forget that some of our favorite ingredients—sunchokes, avocado, pineapple, and chiles are indigenous to the Americas and gifts from our ancestors. This vinaigrette is especially delicious when made with Rancho Gordo's pineapple or banana vinegar (see Sources, page 237).

Spicy and sweet, this vinaigrette makes a fabulous marinade for poultry and game too. Here, it sparks the crunchy jicama and is tempered by the smooth creamy avocado.

Serves 4 to 6

VINAIGRETTE

- 1 jalapeño, seeded and chopped
- ¾ cup small pineapple chunks
- 2 tablespoons honey
- 2 tablespoons vinegar (fruit vinegar preferred)
- ¼ cup extra-virgin olive oil
- Salt

SALAD

- 1 cup cubed jicama
- 1 large avocado, cut into 1-inch chunks
- 2 medium sunchokes, scrubbed and cut into very thin slices
- 1 cup cubed pineapple
- ¼ cup chopped fresh cilantro, for garnish

Vinaigrette: Place the vinaigrette ingredients into a blender or a food processor, and process until smooth.

Salad: Arrange the jicama, avocado, sunchokes, and pineapple on a large serving platter. Drizzle the vinaigrette over all, and garnish with chopped cilantro.

1-2-3 POTATO SALADS

On some of my research adventures through South America, I experienced the glorious wide world of potatoes in thousands of different shapes, sizes, and colors! Their flavors ranged from earthy to peppery to nutty. And I tasted the real difference between a fresh potato and one left to linger and sprout in a plastic bag on the grocer's shelf.

In our family, two different potato salads were always present at our summer get-togethers—family birthday celebrations and holidays, Fourth of July picnics, and random cookouts. The big debate was which of the classic potato salads was the best. One of our sons insisted on yellow, the other on white. The yellow was definitely the winner at the big family picnics. Son Craig preferred the white, so white is what he got! Truth be known, the white is my favorite as well.

At Corn Dance Café, we served both of the "home-styles" along with a tri-colored salad of sweet potatoes, purple potatoes, and white potatoes tossed in a fiery aioli. Try them all!

Mom's Classic Yellow Potato Salad

Ever present on the Corn Dance menu, this was Clay's favorite potato salad. He made sure the dressing was just right (the color of a banana peel) before allowing it to leave the kitchen.

Serves 4 to 6

12 medium to large red potatoes

1 small yellow onion, diced

5 hard-boiled eggs, peeled and diced

¾ cup mayonnaise (such as Hellman's)

3 tablespoons prepared yellow mustard

1 tablespoon whole celery seed

Salt

Put the potatoes into a large pot, and add enough water to cover by about 4 inches. Salt the water so that it tastes like the ocean. Set the pot over high heat, and bring the water to a boil. Then reduce the heat, and simmer until the potatoes are fork tender. Drain. When the potatoes are cool enough to handle, cut them into ½-inch cubes. Place the potatoes, onion, and eggs into a large bowl.

In a small bowl, whisk together the mayonnaise, mustard, and celery seed. Pour this dressing into the bowl with the potatoes, and toss gently to coat. Season with salt to taste.

Craig's White Potato Salad

Here's a classic white potato salad, simple and refined. It's my younger son, Craig's, favorite. It calls for russet potatoes. It is always best to cook russets in chunks rather than whole so they retain their shape. The recipe calls for fresh herbs, but you can also substitute dried fines herbes (see note).

Serves 4 to 6

1½ pounds of russet potatoes, cut into chunks, or fingerlings of uniform sizes

2 tablespoons chopped tarragon

1½ tablespoons chopped parsley

1½ tablespoons chopped chervil

1½ tablespoons chopped chives

½ cup mayonnaise (preferably Hellman's)

1 tablespoon white wine vinegar

Salt

Put the potatoes into a big pot and add enough water to cover by 4 inches and salt to taste. Bring the water to a boil over high heat, then reduce the heat and simmer until the potatoes are tender but still firm, about 10 to 20 minutes, depending on their size. Drain.

In a large bowl, whisk together the tarragon, parsley, chervil, chives, mayonnaise, and vinegar. Put the potatoes into the bowl, and gently toss to coat. Season with salt to taste and adjust the seasonings, adding more herbs as needed.

Note: If you can find a dried fines herbes blend, substitute 1½ tablespoons of that for all the fresh herbs listed above. I'm fond of the Spice Islands brand. If you choose to use the dried blend, add 2 tablespoons of chopped fresh tarragon or 2 teaspoons of dried tarragon, or to taste.

Rainbow Potato Salad

The idea for this salad came to me when I realized how many different kinds of potatoes originated in Peru. We only get a few of the different, colorful varieties in the United States, but that's changing, thanks to the interest in heirloom foods.

Serves 4 to 6

½ pound deep red or purple Peruvian potatoes, cut into 1-inch pieces

½ pound red potatoes, cut into 1-inch pieces

½ pound white or pale-yellow potatoes, cut into 1-inch pieces

3 scallions, sliced

1 tablespoon salt

½ cup mayonnaise (preferably Hellman's)

½ cup sour cream

2 tablespoons Dijon mustard

1 tablespoon cider vinegar

Salt

Put the potatoes into a pot, and add enough water to cover the potatoes by 4 inches. Salt generously, set the pot over high heat, and bring the water to a boil. Reduce the heat, and simmer until the potatoes are tender but retain their shape, about 12 to 15 minutes. Drain.

In a large serving bowl, whisk together the scallions, salt, mayonnaise, mustard, and vinegar. Then add all of the potatoes, and toss gently until they are completely coated. Season to taste with salt. Serve warm, at room temperature, or cold.

TWO GAZPACHOS

Growing up in Oklahoma in the '40s and '50s, the summers were hot, hot, hot. No air conditioning, no cool breezes. But come nightfall, the air would turn velvet and cool down a little. My Grandma and Grandpa Peltier would take my brother and me out to gaze at the stars. Tired from a long day of playing and chasing butterflies, bellies full of delicious meat and gravy, we bedded down in the soft grass on one of Grandma's beautiful quilts. She would point out all of the constellations and tell us their stories. An avid gardener, she could read the moon to know when to plant different seeds. Grandpa would sit, smoke his pipe, and tell an occasional slightly off-color but not too bawdy joke. But Grandma would always shush him by saying, sternly, "Oliver!" while we giggled into our hands.

When cantaloupes and watermelons came into season, we helped Grandma and Grandpa with the harvest and cooled down the melons so they were juicy and refreshing. Worth the wait each year!

Loretta's Gazpacho

I can remember the farmers that would park their pickups, loaded with melons and tomatoes, at strategic intersections to sell.

This refreshing soup is the taste of summer in a bowl, and it just brims with the flavors of the Southwest. Be sure to chill it for a couple of hours or overnight before serving. It's especially pretty served with blue corn chips.

Serves 4 to 6

1½ pounds tomatoes, quartered and cored

2 cloves garlic

3 jalapeños, quartered, seeded, and deveined

4 tomatillos, husked, quartered lengthwise, and cored

1 red onion, finely chopped

1 green bell pepper, seeded, and finely chopped

1 red bell pepper, seeded, and finely chopped

2 cups fresh corn kernels

3 cups tomato juice (not V-8 Juice)

2 tablespoons fresh lime juice

2 teaspoons salt

½ cup chopped cilantro

Put the tomatoes into a food processor, and pulse until they're coarsely chopped. Transfer the tomatoes to a nonreactive bowl.

Place the garlic, jalapeños, and tomatillos into the food processor, and pulse until minced. Add this mixture to the tomatoes.

Add the onions and bell peppers to the tomato mixture along with the corn, tomato juice, lime juice, and salt. Stir to combine, taste, and adjust the seasonings. Stir in the cilantro. Cover the bowl, and chill for at least 2 hours before serving.

Watermelon Gazpacho

On Highland Street, near Van's Pig Stand, was Ragg's BBQ, where farmers sold watermelon from a big red Coca-Cola cooler filled with ice. You'd pick out a melon, and Ragg would cut out a "plug" so you could taste it. We'd choose our melon, then sit nearby at a long wooden table savoring each sweet, drippy bite.

This cold soup relies on yellow watermelon and yellow tomatoes, but feel free to substitute red watermelon and red tomatoes. Serve the soup icy cold!

Serves 4 to 6

- 2 cups seeded or seedless cubed yellow watermelon, plus more for garnish
- 2 cups orange juice
- 4 tablespoons extra-virgin olive oil
- 1 seedless cucumber, cut into ¼-inch dice
- 2 tomatoes, chopped
- 1 small jalapeño, seeded, deveined, and minced
- 1 small yellow bell pepper, seeded and diced
- 1 small onion, cut into ¼-inch dice
- 2 cloves garlic, minced
- 2 tablespoons fresh lime juice
- 2 tablespoons chopped fresh basil, plus more for garnish
- 2 tablespoons chopped fresh mint, plus more for garnish
- 2 tablespoons of chopped cilantro, plus more for garnish
- Salt

Process ½ cup of the watermelon, the orange juice, and 2 tablespoons of the oil in a blender until pureed. Transfer to a large bowl.

Stir in the remaining watermelon cubes, cucumber, tomatoes, jalapeño, bell pepper, onion, garlic, lime juice, remaining 2 tablespoons of the oil, and herbs. Cover with plastic, and chill for at least 2 hours. Season with salt to taste before serving. Garnish the soup with more watermelon and chopped fresh herbs.

Kanuchi

Many southeastern tribes have their own version of kanuchi, a thick nut soup that is traditionally served over hominy. Years ago, nutmeat paste would be shaped into softball-sized hunks and stored in wood barrels or clay pots to be used for making this soup and thickening stews throughout the winter.

In this recipe, a food processor transforms the nuts into a paste (saving the time of pounding). It's made with the simplest ingredients, so the taste of these nuts shines through. You'll end up with more nut paste than needed for the soup, but it stores beautifully for up to a month and may be frozen.

Serves 4 to 6

- 4 ounces raw hickory nuts, pecans, or a mix of walnuts and pecans
- 1 quart cold water
- 1 teaspoon salt, or more to taste
- 1 tablespoon maple syrup, or more to taste
- 1 cup cooked and drained whole or cracked hominy (see Hominy, page 117), or 1 sweet potato, roasted, peeled, and cut into ½-inch dice (see note)

In a food processor fitted with a steel blade, process the nuts, scraping down the sides once or twice, to form a thick paste, about 3 minutes. Scrape the nut paste into a large stockpot, and add the water and salt. Set the pot over high heat and bring the water to a boil, whisking the nut paste until it dissolves and the liquid thickens. Reduce the heat and simmer uncovered, stirring often, until the liquid is reduced by half, about 30 minutes.

Stir in the maple syrup, increase the heat, and bring the mixture to a boil, cooking until any separated fats on the surface have emulsified back into the soup. Taste and adjust the seasonings. Serve warm over hominy or roasted sweet potatoes.

Note: Preheat the oven to 350 degrees. Score a large X in the center of the sweet potato, and place it on a baking sheet. Roast until tender, about 45 to 50 minutes. Remove, and allow to cool enough to handle. Peel the sweet potato, and mash the flesh or cut it into cubes.

Three Sisters Stew with Corn Dumplings

I love dumplings! I created these to showcase good-quality cornmeal: they have more flavor and are more nutritious (and much prettier) than dumplings made with white flour. Try them in other soups and stews!

Originally from the Corn Dance Café menu, the dish is now a hit at Thirty Nine Restaurant. Leftovers will keep 3 days in a covered container in the refrigerator or may be frozen. If you're in a pinch, use canned beans, but the freshly cooked are, oh, so much better!

Serves 6 to 8

STEW

- 2 cups mixed dried beans (Anasazi or pinto, lima, white, and black), soaked overnight
- 1 tablespoon olive oil
- 1½ cups finely chopped yellow onion
- 1½ cups finely chopped green bell pepper
- 2 tablespoons finely chopped garlic
- 1 jalapeño, seeded and finely chopped
- 2 teaspoons cumin seed
- ⅛ teaspoon cayenne pepper
- 2 teaspoons chili powder
- 1 (28-ounce) can crushed tomatoes, with juice
- 2 quarts Best Vegetable Stock (page 68) or water
- 3 cups corn kernels
- ½ cup dark beer
- 2 cups diced zucchini or yellow squash
- Salt

DUMPLINGS

- ¾ cup blue or yellow cornmeal
- ¼ cup all-purpose flour
- 2 teaspoons baking powder
- ½ teaspoon salt
- 1 egg
- ⅓ cup milk
- 1 tablespoon unsalted butter, melted
- ½ cup corn kernels

Stew: After soaking the beans overnight, drain them and set them aside.

Heat the oil in a large deep stockpot or Dutch oven set over medium-high heat, and add the onions, bell pepper, garlic, and jalapeño. Cook until soft, about 5 minutes.

In a dry skillet, toast the cumin seeds until they're aromatic and lightly browned, about 30 seconds. Grind the seeds in a mini food processor or a coffee or spice grinder, and add them to the onion mixture.

In the same dry skillet, toast the cayenne and chili powder for about 30 seconds, being careful not to burn them. Add the toasted spices to the onion mixture in the stockpot.

Stir the tomatoes into the stockpot, and simmer for about 15 minutes. Add the stock and the drained beans to the pot, and bring the stock to a boil. Reduce the heat, cover, and simmer until the beans are tender, about 1½ to 2 hours.

Stir in the corn, beer, and squash, and cook until the squash is tender, about 10 minutes. Season with salt to taste.

Dumplings: Stir together the cornmeal, flour, baking powder, and salt in a medium bowl. In a separate bowl, whisk together the egg, milk, and melted butter. Add the liquid to the dry ingredients, and mix until just combined. Fold in the corn. Drop the batter by heaping tablespoons into the simmering stew. (There should be about 16 dumplings.) Cover and cook until a wooden toothpick inserted into the centers of the dumplings comes up clean, about 15 minutes.

Spoon the soup into bowls, making sure to scoop 2 dumplings into each bowl. Serve immediately.

Butternut Squash Soup with Frizzled Sage and Toasted Squash Seeds

This soup relies on the quality of the squash and is remarkably easy to make. Feel free to substitute roasted sweet potatoes or pumpkin. Serve with Pumpkin Cream Biscuits (page 159) topped with Loretta's Fierce Tomato Jam (page 219).

Serves 4 to 6

1 large butternut squash (about 3 pounds), halved lengthwise and seeded

1 teaspoon maple syrup or honey, or more to taste

3 to 4 cups Best Vegetable Stock (page 68)

Cilantro oil (see note) or chili oil, for garnish

1 cup frizzled sage leaves (see note), for garnish

¼ cup toasted squash seeds (see note), for garnish

Preheat the oven to 425 degrees. Line a rimmed baking sheet with parchment paper. Place the butternut squash on the pan, and drizzle the cut sides with just enough oil to lightly coat the squash. Sprinkle with salt.

Place the squash cut-side down, and roast until tender and cooked through, about 40 to 50 minutes. Set the squash aside to cool.

Scoop the butternut squash flesh into the blender, and discard the tough skin. Taste and sweeten with a touch of maple syrup or honey and season. Pour in 3 cups of the vegetable broth, being careful not to overfill; work in batches if necessary. Taste, and add maple syrup and salt to taste.

Puree the soup on high, and turn the puree back into the soup pot. Taste and adjust the seasonings, and add more stock as needed. Heat the soup over medium heat for about 15 minutes. Serve the soup hot and garnished with a swirl of cilantro oil, crumbled frizzled sage leaves, and toasted squash seeds.

Notes:

• Frizzled sage leaves: Film a small skillet with a little oil and set it over medium-high heat. Lightly fry the leaves, being careful not to crowd the pan, until crisp, about 1 to 2 minutes. Drain the sage on a paper towel.

• Toasted squash seeds: Preheat the oven to 375 degrees, and line a baking sheet with parchment paper. Rinse the squash seeds under cold running water, and clean them of any clinging squash. Pat the seeds thoroughly dry on cloth or paper towels. Toss the seeds in enough olive oil to lightly coat, scatter them over the baking sheet, and sprinkle with coarse salt. Roast until they're lightly browned and crisped. Remove, and allow to cool before storing in an airtight container.

• Cilantro oil: In a food processor fitted with a steel blade, puree ¼ cup of cilantro leaves with ½ cup of olive oil. Strain the oil into a small bowl or jar with a lid. Store the oil in a covered container in the refrigerator, and use within 4 days.

BASKET SOUP

Many of our ancestors relied on this innovative method of cooking soups and stews before the advent of metal cookware. They filled beautiful, tightly woven baskets with ingredients. Then, to bring the soup to a boil, they dropped hot rocks—lifted from the fire and rinsed of ash—into the soup to bring it to a boil.

The key was to take care and pay attention when stirring the soup. Stir too vigorously and the basket would wear out before the soup was finished; stir too slowly and the basket might burn. It was said that a man seeking a wife checked her baskets to see whether they were torn or burned as a way of judging her ability to make good meals.

Best Vegetable Stock

This recipe calls for roasting the vegetables first to enrich the flavor of the stock. It's perfect for vegetable-centric soups, sauces, and stews. It's also wonderful on its own with a side of cornbread.

Makes about 2 quarts

3 large yellow onions, peeled and cut into 2-inch chunks

3 carrots, cut into 2-inch chunks

2 to 3 celery stalks, cut into 2-inch chunks

3 plum tomatoes (or other tomatoes), cut into 2-inch chunks

2 cloves garlic

2 tablespoons extra-virgin olive oil

1 bay leaf

6 sprigs fresh thyme

1 sprig sage

2 sprigs oregano

Preheat the oven to 450 degrees. Scatter the onions, carrots, celery, tomatoes, and garlic on a baking sheet, and drizzle them with olive oil. Roast until the vegetables are nicely browned, about 25 to 30 minutes, shaking the pan occasionally. Remove the vegetables, and put them into a deep pot. Add enough water to cover the vegetables by about 1 inch. Add the bay leaf, thyme, sage, and oregano to the pot.

Set the pot over high heat and bring the stock to a boil, then reduce the heat and simmer for about 2 hours. Allow the stock to cool. Set a strainer over a bowl, and pour the stock and vegetables into the strainer, pressing with the back of a spoon. Discard the vegetables. Store the stock in a covered container in the refrigerator for up to a week, or freeze it.

Corn Stock

Never ever throw away corn cobs! They are the base for fabulous corn soups and stews. You can make corn stock for A-Maizing Corn Ice Cream (page 182) and other desserts by omitting the onion.

Makes about 4 cups

1 onion, peeled and quartered

6 corn cobs, kernels removed and reserved for another use

Place the onion, corn cobs, and 2 quarts of water into a medium saucepan. Set the pan over high heat to bring the water to a boil, then reduce the heat and simmer for 45 minutes. Remove the pot from the heat, and discard the onion and corn cobs. Allow the stock to cool before storing it in a covered container for up to one week or freezing it.

Golden Corn Soup

The secret to this silky, creamless corn soup is scraping the corn milk (juices) from the cob. Serve the soup with a swirl of cilantro oil.

Serves about 4 to 6

4 ears sweet corn, husked

¼ cup corn oil or sunflower oil

1 tablespoon corn flour

1 sweet onion, thinly sliced

Coarse salt

Dash cayenne pepper

Dash turmeric

4 cups Corn Stock (this page) or Best Vegetable Stock (page 68)

Cilantro oil (see note on page 65), for garnish

To remove the kernels and milk from the corn, stand the cob tip up in a medium bowl. Use a sharp knife to cut the kernels from the cob into the bowl, and then drag the back of the knife down the cob to release the corn milk into the bowl.

Film a large saucepan with the oil, and set it over medium heat. Add the onion and a pinch of salt and cook, stirring, until the onion is softened, about 5 minutes. Add the corn flour with the cayenne and turmeric, and cook for 1 minute. Stir in the corn kernels with their milk and 2 cups of the stock. Reduce the heat, and simmer until the corn kernels are tender, about 6 to 8 minutes. Remove the soup from the heat, and transfer it to a blender. Working in small batches, puree the corn mixture until it is very smooth, about 2 minutes. Do not process all of the hot soup at once; hot ingredients can explode out of the blender! Serve the soup warm, or refrigerate and serve it cold. Garnish the soup with a swirl of cilantro oil.

Fields and Forests

Blue Corn Pancakes, Sweet and Savory 73

Mushroom Frittata with Peppers
and Goat Cheese 74

Chile Cheese Casserole 76

Black Bean, Corn, and Sweet Potato Chili 77

Creamy Grits with Roasted Squash 80

Wild Forest Mushrooms and Sun-Dried
Tomatoes on Corn Pasta 82

Wild Rice, Quinoa, and Cranberry
Stuffed Squash 83

Stuffed Portobellos 84

Roasted-Garlic Mashed Potatoes 85

I was blessed with the best teachers—my Mother, Grandmothers, Great Grandmothers, and Aunties. The kitchen, garden, and fields were my classrooms; their kitchens, my laboratories. We harvested young poke, lambsquarters, dandelions, and other wild greens in the spring and later, lush garden tomatoes, sweet corn, potatoes, and all sorts of beans. I remember those pots of beans, simmered until creamy, for hearty soups and stews paired with cornbread. Sometimes they were seasoned with hunks of salt pork or ham hocks but often, lacking access to meat, they were what we'd now call vegetarian or vegan. The dining world has caught up with those of us who grew up eating mostly plants.

Blue Corn Pancakes, Sweet and Savory

We serve these pancakes for breakfast piled with fresh local berries and maple syrup. For lunch or dinner, they're chocked with jalapeños and plenty of sweet corn and garnished with pesto or chopped herbs.

Serves 6 to 8

1 cup fine-ground yellow cornmeal

½ cup stone-ground blue cornmeal

½ cup all-purpose flour

2 teaspoons sugar

2 teaspoons baking powder

1 teaspoon baking soda

Salt

1¾ cups buttermilk

6 tablespoons unsalted butter, melted

2 large eggs

½ cup corn kernels

Vegetable oil for frying

Preheat the oven to 250 degrees, and line a baking sheet with parchment paper. In a large bowl, stir together the cornmeal, flour, sugar, baking powder, baking soda, and a generous pinch of salt.

In a medium bowl, whisk together the buttermilk, butter, and eggs, and then stir in the corn. Turn the buttermilk mixture into the dry ingredients, and mix with a rubber spatula just until moistened.

Heat 1 tablespoon of the oil in a large sauté pan over medium heat. Using a ¼-cup measuring cup, drop the batter onto the pan, being careful not to crowd the pancakes. Cook until bubbles begin to form on top of the pancakes and the bottom begins to brown, about 1 to 2 minutes. Turn the pancakes, and cook the second side until the pancakes seem firm and the second side is browned. Using a spatula, place the pancakes on the baking sheet and put them into the oven to keep warm until the rest of the pancakes have been cooked. Serve warm.

Savory variation: Omit the sugar. Seed and mince a small jalapeño, and add it to the batter along with the corn.

Mushroom Frittata with Peppers and Goat Cheese

A delicious breakfast and a wonderful lunch dish, this frittata comes together quickly. Serve it warm or make it ahead of time and serve it at room temperature. It's great with Chipotle Mayonnaise (page 223) or your favorite salsa.

Serves 4 to 6

2 tablespoons extra-virgin olive oil

10 ounces fresh mushrooms (a mix of cremini, shiitake, and any wild mushrooms)

1 large shallot, minced

Salt

1 small red bell pepper, seeded and diced

8 eggs

3 ounces goat cheese

4 to 6 tablespoons Chipotle Mayonnaise (page 223)

In a 10-inch non-stick skillet, heat 1 tablespoon of the oil over medium. Add the mushrooms and the shallot with a pinch of salt. Sauté, turning occasionally, until they release their juices, about 3 to 5 minutes. Stir in the peppers, and continue cooking until the peppers are limp, another 3 to 5 minutes. Remove the pan from the heat.

In a medium bowl, beat the eggs and season them with salt. Stir in the sautéed vegetables.

Wipe the pan clean, add the remaining tablespoon of oil to the pan, and set pan over medium-high heat. Pour the egg mixture into the pan, and swirl the pan to distribute the eggs over the entire surface. Shake the pan, then tilt it while lifting the frittata's edges with a spatula to let the eggs run underneath. Once a few layers of egg have cooked, reduce the heat and drop spoonfuls of the goat cheese over the frittata. Cover the skillet, and let the eggs cook. To loosen the bottom of the frittata and keep it from burning, occasionally shake the pan gently and remove the lid to loosen the bottom of the frittata with the spatula. Cook until the eggs are just set, about 10 minutes. While the eggs are cooking, preheat the broiler.

Uncover the pan, and place it under the broiler to set the top of the frittata. Remove the pan from the broiler, and allow the frittata to cool for about 5 minutes. To serve, cut the frittata into wedges and top each with a dollop of Chipotle Mayonnaise.

Potato variation: Omit the mushrooms. Boil and slice 8 to 10 red or Yukon Gold potatoes, and line the skillet with them. Pour the beaten eggs and peppers over the potatoes, and set the skillet on the stove over a medium-low flame. Cover and cook as directed in the recipe until the eggs are just set. Add the goat cheese, and then run the skillet under the broiler until the top of the frittata is set.

Chile Cheese Casserole

We serve this casserole Christmas morning or anytime we're hosting a hearty brunch; it's a hit at potlucks.

Serves 4 to 6

2 (4-ounce) cans diced green chiles

2 cups shredded mixed cheeses (such as Monterey Jack, Colby, and Cheddar)

1 cup sour cream

3 eggs

Salt

Hot sauce (optional)

Preheat the oven to 350 degrees. Lightly grease an 8 × 8 inch baking dish. Line the dish with half the chiles, then cover the chiles with half of the shredded cheese. Cover the cheese layer with the rest of the chiles and then the rest of the cheese.

In a small bowl, beat the eggs with the sour cream, and season them with salt and several shots of hot sauce, if using. Spread the egg mixture over the cheese layer, then poke holes into the casserole so the egg mixture drips through. Bake until the top of the casserole is nicely browned and the eggs are set, about 30 to 40 minutes.

Black Bean, Corn, and Sweet Potato Chili

This hearty vegetarian chili comes together in a snap, and then simmers away on its own without asking much of the cook. Switch out the sweet potato for squash. The chipotles give this chili a smoky heat. Serve it with big hunks of Corn Dance Cornbread (page 153).

Serves 4 to 6

¼ cup olive oil or sunflower oil

1 large onion, finely chopped

Pinch salt

7 cloves garlic, smashed and chopped

3 teaspoons ground cumin

2 tablespoons lime juice

1 to 4 canned chipotles in adobo, finely chopped, plus a little adobo sauce to taste

1½ pounds sweet potatoes, scrubbed and cut into 1-inch pieces

1½ cups dried black beans, soaked overnight and cooked (see note on page 28), or 4 cups canned black beans, drained and rinsed

1 (28-ounce) can fire-roasted diced tomatoes with their juice

Salt

2 cups corn kernels

Sliced avocado, for garnish

Thinly sliced red onion, for garnish

Chopped cilantro, for garnish

1 lime, cut into wedges, for garnish

In a large Dutch oven, warm the oil over medium-high heat. Add the onion, season with salt, and cook, stirring occasionally, until the onion is translucent, about 5 minutes. Add the garlic and cook, stirring, until it's fragrant, about 1 minute. Stir in the cumin, then add the lime juice, chipotles, adobo sauce, sweet potatoes, beans, and tomatoes. Season with salt, then add about 1 cup of water and bring it to a boil. Reduce the heat to low and simmer, covered, until the sweet potatoes are tender, about 30 to 40 minutes. Stir in the corn. Taste, and adjust the seasonings. Garnish the chili with avocado, red onion, and cilantro, and serve it with lime wedges on the side.

GRITS, NOT JUST FOR BREAKFAST

Grits are ground dried white or yellow corn. The best grits are stone-ground, the old-fashioned way, leaving much of the flavor and nutrients intact. The term *grits* refers to the coarsest grind of corn; polenta is less coarse, and corn flour is even finer. Be sure to keep stone-ground grits in the refrigerator or freezer, as you would any fresh food.

Creamy Grits with Roasted Squash

Here's the kind of dish that is fabulous any time of day—serve it for brunch, lunch, or dinner. I crown this vegetarian dish with golden nuggets of roasted winter squash. Drizzle the whole thing with a little Hot Honey (page 222) for a fabulous finish. The grits are also fantastic topped with the Spicy Houma Shrimp (page 105) and as a bed for Braised Bison Short Ribs (page 135).

Serves 4 to 6

1 small butternut squash, peeled and cut into 2-inch pieces

2 tablespoons extra-virgin olive oil

Coarse salt

1 tablespoon chopped sage

1 teaspoon salt

1 cup white corn grits

1 tablespoon Hot Honey (page 222), plus more for serving

Toasted squash seeds (see note on page 65), for garnish

Preheat the oven to 400 degrees, and line a baking sheet with parchment paper.

Scatter the squash over the baking sheet, and toss it with the oil. Sprinkle the squash with salt and the sage. Roast the squash, shaking the pan occasionally, until it's nicely browned along the edges, about 15 to 20 minutes. Pull the squash from the oven, and brush it with 1 tablespoon of the Hot Honey. Return the pan to the oven for 3 to 4 minutes to glaze the squash.

Prepare the grits while the squash roasts. Bring 3 cups of water to a boil in a large saucepan set over medium heat. Whisk in the teaspoon of salt, then slowly sprinkle the grits into the water, whisking constantly. Reduce to a simmer, continue whisking, and cook until the grits have opened and no longer taste raw, about 5 to 10 minutes. Remove the grits from the heat, and set them aside to rest.

Serve the grits topped with a drizzle of Hot Honey, the roasted squash, and toasted squash seeds.

Wild Forest Mushrooms and Sun-Dried Tomatoes on Corn Pasta

I like using corn pasta as an alternative to wheat pasta. It's a lush golden color with a nuanced corn flavor. Corn pasta cooks quickly, so keep an eye on the pot as it simmers. In this recipe, use a mix of mushrooms for varied texture and flavor. Be sure to serve this dish with a generous drizzle of Creamed Garlic (page 226).

Serves 4 to 6

8 to 10 ounces corn pasta

2 tablespoons extra-virgin olive oil

10 ounces mixed mushrooms (cremini, shiitake, or wild varieties, such as chanterelles, morels, wood ear, and lion's mane), sliced (see note)

½ cup dry white wine

½ cup diced sun-dried tomatoes

5 cloves garlic

1 cup vegetable stock

3 tablespoons fresh basil

2 cups spinach or chopped kale

Salt

¼ cup Creamed Garlic (page 226)

Get a big pot of water boiling over high heat, and add enough salt that it tastes like the ocean. Drop in the pasta, and cook until it's just tender, about 6 to 8 minutes. Drain.

Heat the oil in a large skillet over medium-high heat. Sauté the mushrooms, then cover and cook until they release their juices, about 5 to 8 minutes. Remove the lid, reduce the heat slightly, and continue cooking until the mushrooms are dark. Stir in the wine, tomatoes, and garlic, and cook until the garlic has softened. Stir in the stock, and simmer to reduce by half. Stir in the basil and the greens, then toss the pasta into the skillet. Season with salt, then serve topped with a dollop of Creamed Garlic.

Note: Many farmers markets, co-ops, and grocery stores sell foraged and cultivated wild mushrooms. They add great variety to our mushroom recipes and are a safe way to enjoy mushrooms without the uncertainty of foraging yourself. Many foragers and universities offer guided wild mushroom experiences that are worth checking out if you want to try foraging.

Wild Rice, Quinoa, and Cranberry Stuffed Squash

Acorn squash serves as the vessel for this handsome, healthful dish of indigenous grains. Brilliant cranberries add pops of color and tang. It makes a hearty side dish to roast game and a fine vegetarian meal. If you like, skip the squash and shape the grain mixture into pretty timbales.

Acorn squash ranges in size; for this dish, look for smaller squash. Each half will be a single serving.

Serves 6

3 small acorn squash, cut in half crosswise and seeded

3 tablespoons extra-virgin olive oil

2 cups quinoa

1 cup hand-harvested wild rice

¾ teaspoon salt

4 green onions, trimmed and chopped

¼ cup dried cranberries, coarsely chopped

¼ cup pecans or walnuts, coarsely chopped

¼ cup chicken or vegetable stock

Preheat the oven to 350 degrees. Season the cavities and cut sides of the squash with salt, and brush them with olive oil. Place the squash cut-side down on a baking sheet, and cover it tightly with foil. Bake until the squash gives just a little, about 30 minutes. Remove the squash from the oven, and set it aside.

Rinse the quinoa thoroughly. Bring 4 cups of water to boil in a large pot, and add the quinoa and ¼ teaspoon of the salt. Reduce the heat, cover, and simmer on medium-low until the quinoa's germ, or tail, appears, about 12 to 15 minutes. Remove from the heat, and let the quinoa rest for 5 minutes before fluffing it with a fork.

Rinse the wild rice thoroughly until the water runs clear. Place the rice, 3 cups of water, and ½ teaspoon of salt in a large pot. Bring the water to a boil. Reduce the heat, cover, and simmer just until the wild rice blossoms, about 20 to 25 minutes. Drain and set aside.

Film a medium skillet with the remaining oil, and set it over medium heat. Sauté the onions until they're tender, about 5 to 10 minutes. Put the quinoa, wild rice, onions, cranberries, and nuts into a large bowl. Add the stock and stir to combine. Taste the grain mixture, and adjust the seasoning.

Turn the squash cut-side up on the baking sheet, and spoon in the grain mixture. Cover the pan with aluminum foil. Bake until the squash is very tender, about 20 minutes. Remove the foil, and continue baking until the tops are nicely browned, about 10 minutes. Serve hot or warm.

Stuffed Portobellos

These generously stuffed portobello mushrooms will satisfy hungry vegans and omnivores alike. The hearty blend of white beans, wild rice, and quinoa comes together quickly, and the recipe is easily doubled for a crowd.

To get the best "mushroom" flavor from the portobellos, be sure to scrape out the gills inside the mushroom using a teaspoon to remove any grit, dirt, and moisture.

Serves 4 to 6

- 6 large portobello mushrooms, stems removed and gills scraped clean
- 1 tablespoon extra-virgin olive oil
- ¾ teaspoon coarse salt, plus extra for the mushrooms
- ½ cup dried tepary or white beans, soaked overnight, or 1 cup drained and rinsed canned beans
- 1 cup quinoa
- ½ cup wild rice
- 1 small onion, finely chopped
- 1 small red bell pepper, seeded and diced
- 2 cloves garlic, finely chopped
- 1 teaspoon chopped sage
- ¼ cup vegetable stock

Preheat the oven to 375 degrees. Line a baking sheet with parchment paper, and place the mushroom caps on it upside down. Brush the mushrooms with the oil, and season them with salt. Bake until tender, about 15 minutes to 20 minutes.

Place the beans in a large saucepan. Add enough water to cover the beans by 4 inches. Set the saucepan over high heat, and bring the water to a boil. Reduce the heat, and simmer the beans, covered, until they're tender, about 1 to 1½ hours for tepary beans, 30 to 45 minutes for white beans. Drain the beans.

Rinse the quinoa thoroughly. Bring 2 cups of water to boil in a small pot, and add the quinoa and ¼ teaspoon of salt. Reduce the heat, cover, and simmer on medium-low until the quinoa's germ, or tail, appears, about 12 to 15 minutes. Remove from the heat, and let the quinoa rest for 5 minutes before fluffing it with a fork.

Rinse the wild rice thoroughly until the water runs clear. Place the rice, 3 cups of water, and ½ teaspoon of salt in a large pot. Bring the water to a boil. Reduce the heat, cover, and simmer just until the wild rice blossoms, about 20 to 25 minutes. Drain and set aside.

Film a large skillet with the remaining oil, and set it over medium heat. Add the onion, bell pepper, and garlic, and cook until they're beginning to brown. Season with more salt, and then stir in the sage, beans, quinoa, wild rice, and stock. Divide the mixture among the mushroom caps. Return them to the oven, and bake until they're thoroughly heated through, about 10 minutes. Serve hot.

Roasted-Garlic Mashed Potatoes

Golden potatoes whipped with sweet, mellow roasted garlic are rich and creamy, without the use of cream and butter. This recipe relies on great olive oil to do most of the work. These potatoes make a fabulous side dish and are hearty enough for a simple dinner when paired with a crisp salad.

Serves 4

1 head garlic

¼ cup good-quality olive oil

2 pounds yellow potatoes (Yukon Gold or German Butterball), cut into 1-inch chunks

Salt

Preheat the oven to 400 degrees. Peel and discard the papery outer layers from the whole garlic bulb, leaving intact the skins of the individual cloves. Using a sharp knife, cut ¼ inch from the top of the garlic bulb to expose the tips of the individual cloves. Place the garlic upright in a 6-inch square of aluminum foil. Drizzle a couple of teaspoons over oil the exposed cloves, using your fingers to rub in the oil. Fold the foil up around the head of garlic, and bake it until the garlic is very tender and the skins are caramelized, about 30 to 40 minutes. Remove the garlic from the oven, and set it aside.

Bring a large saucepan of water to a boil, add the potatoes and a generous pinch of salt, and cook at a brisk simmer until the potatoes are very tender. Drain the potatoes, reserving 1 cup of the cooking liquid. Return the potatoes to the pot. Beat in the remaining oil. Squeeze the cloves from the head of roasted garlic into the potatoes, and whisk until you've reached the desired consistency. Add salt to taste.

Wide Oceans, Deep Lakes, Fast Rivers

FISH AND SHELLFISH

Salmon Croquettes with
Horseradish Sauce 89

Smoked Oyster Cakes 90

Spiced Griddled Salmon 92

Cedar-Planked Salmon 92

Mint-Stuffed Roast Lake Trout 93

Best Fried Fish 94

Hush Puppies 95

Mudbug Stew 98

Shellfish Stock 99

Mussels and Chanterelles
Simmered with Pine Needles 101

Spicy Houma Shrimp 105

On family camping trips, Dad excelled at making shore lunch. He'd clean the fish we'd just caught, adjust the fire to get the oil bubbling hot, then flash fry the fillets until they were crispy and light. Through the years, as we taped *Seasoned with Spirit*, I've walked beaches hunting mussels, cooked wild salmon over open grills, and stirred up fiery stews of Houma shrimp and crawfish, tasting the gifts of our Native waters. The best of these dishes I share here with you.

Salmon Croquettes with Horseradish Sauce

When I was a child, I'd help Grandma Peltier (my Mom's Mom) in the kitchen. She'd turn a chair backward for me to stand on so I could reach the countertop. She'd tie the pretty flowered apron she sewed for me around my waist. I'd crush saltines between sheets of waxed paper for the salmon croquettes and then crack the eggs into a bowl. Back then, we used canned salmon, and I was amazed that we could eat the bones!

This recipe makes great use of leftover cooked or smoked salmon or trout, but canned salmon still works nicely. Serve the croquettes with Loretta's Fierce Tomato Jam (page 219) or any of the salsas in the chapter "Preserving the Best," plus a dollop of Horseradish Sauce.

Serves 4 to 6

CROQUETTES

- 2 (15-ounce) cans salmon, drained and cleaned, liquid reserved; or 30 ounces leftover cooked or smoked salmon or trout
- 1 cup crushed saltine crackers
- 1 large egg
- ¼ cup finely chopped cilantro or parsley
  Vegetable oil for frying

HORSERADISH SAUCE

- ½ cup good-quality mayonnaise (such as Hellman's)
- ¼ cup whole-milk Greek yogurt
- 1 to 2 tablespoons prepared fresh horseradish

Croquettes: In a large bowl, flake the salmon and add ⅔ cup of the crushed crackers, the egg, and the cilantro. Stir well, then form the mixture into 8 croquettes. Spread the remaining cracker crumbs out in a shallow dish, and dredge the croquettes in the crumbs. Place the croquettes on a parchment paper–lined plate and refrigerate them for 1 to 2 hours.

In a deep skillet, heat about 4 inches of oil over high heat until it shimmers and reaches about 350 degrees on a candy thermometer. Working in batches, fry the croquettes until they're browned, about 6 to 7 minutes per side. Drain the croquettes on a paper towel, and serve them with Loretta's Fierce Tomato Jam or salsa and a dollop of the Horseradish Sauce.

Horseradish Sauce: In a small bowl, whisk together the mayonnaise, yogurt, and horseradish. Store in a covered container in the refrigerator for up to one week.

Smoked Oyster Cakes

These crispy cakes make a wonderful side to Spiced Griddled Salmon (page 92) and are a simple light meal on their own. Serve them drizzled with Rose Hip Sauce (page 229) or Mom's Famous Chile Sauce (Piccalilli) (page 216). The oyster cakes are great paired with a fresh, crunchy, very simple veggie slaw.

Serves 6

12 to 15 small red potatoes, scrubbed and quartered

10 smoked oysters, canned or freshly smoked (see note), coarsely chopped

1 egg

½ cup thinly sliced scallions

1 teaspoon chopped fresh thyme

Salt

Flour for dusting the cakes

2 to 3 tablespoons olive oil

Put the potatoes into a deep pot with enough water to cover the potatoes by 4 inches. Add a generous pinch of salt. Set the pot over high heat, bring the water to a boil, and cook the potatoes until they're very tender, about 15 to 20 minutes. Drain most of the water from the potatoes, leaving about ½ inch in the bottom of the pot. With a potato masher, smash the potatoes. Set the potatoes aside to cool.

In a medium bowl, work together the oysters, 2 cups of the mashed potatoes, egg, scallions, thyme, and salt to make a thick dough. Lightly flour your hands. Scoop up spoonfuls of the dough and, using your hands, gently pat them into cakes. Lightly cover a plate with flour, and dust the cakes with flour on both sides.

Heat the oil over medium until it ripples. Working in batches so as not to crowd the pan, brown the cakes until they develop a crust and are heated through, about 5 minutes per side.

Note: I smoke fresh oysters on the half shell over sassafras, hickory, mesquite, apple, or cherry wood. These woods infuse a deliciously different smoky flavor. But canned smoked oysters will work too.

Spiced Griddled Salmon

Spiked with smoky, warm flavors, this griddled salmon is perfect when finished with a drizzle of Rose Hip Sauce (page 229). Store any extra sauce in a covered container in the refrigerator to drizzle over roast chicken. The salmon is great paired with Smoked Oyster Cakes (page 90).

Serves 4

4 salmon fillets (about 4 ounces each), skin on

3 tablespoons extra-virgin olive oil

¼ teaspoon ancho chile powder

⅛ teaspoon ground cumin

½ teaspoon maple sugar or brown sugar

Lay the salmon skin-side down on a plate or a baking sheet, and brush it with generous amounts of the oil. Sprinkle the fish with the ancho chile powder, cumin, and sugar. Pour the remaining oil into a large skillet, and set the skillet over medium-high heat. Set the fillets skin-side down in the pan, and cook until the skin releases from the bottom of the pan, about 2 to 3 minutes. Flip the fillets, and continue cooking until the internal temperature reaches 120 degrees on an instant-read thermometer, another 2 to 3 minutes. Serve drizzled with Rose Hip Sauce (page 229).

Cedar-Planked Salmon

This is a traditional method of cooking salmon on the Northwest Coast. The salmon takes on the flavors of wood and smoke when set on a cedar plank and grilled over a low flame. Serve the salmon with fire-roasted potatoes or Smoked Oyster Cakes (page 90).

You can buy cedar planks in specialty shops and online. I prefer untreated cedar shingles from the lumber yard; I just cut them to size.

Serves 6

1 cedar plank, about 16 inches long

1 tablespoon extra-virgin olive oil

2 tablespoons maple syrup

1 teaspoon minced mint

1 tablespoon grated lemon zest

1 (2-pound) salmon fillet with skin on, about 1½ inches thick

Immerse the cedar plank in enough water to cover it. Let it soak for about 2 hours.

Prepare a grill or preheat a gas grill to medium-high.

In a small bowl, whisk together the olive oil, maple syrup, mint, and lemon zest. Spread this mixture over the flesh side of the salmon.

Put the salmon on the plank, skin-side down. Set the plank on the grill, cover with the lid, and cook until the salmon flakes and separates easily along the white lines that run across the fillet and is browned on the edges, about 13 to 15 minutes. Let the salmon stand a few minutes before serving.

Mint-Stuffed Roast Lake Trout

If you're lucky enough to catch (or purchase) a big, 4- to 6-pound lake trout, you're in for a real treat. A whole fish stuffed with mint makes a gorgeous presentation. Serve this big catch on a platter, and allow people to slice off chunks themselves. Serve the trout over wild rice with Tangy Sauce for Fish (page 226), Rose Hip Sauce (page 229), or Sweet Corn Vinaigrette (page 50).

Although this recipe calls for roasting the trout, grilling the trout over wood works well too. The wood gives the fish a wonderfully smoky flavor. Be careful to keep the heat low and even so the trout does not burn but cooks all the way through.

Serves about 4 to 6

Extra-virgin olive oil

Salt

1 big lake trout, about 4 to 6 pounds

2 lemons, thinly sliced

8 fresh sprigs mint

8 fresh sprigs parsley

1 medium tart apple, cored and thinly sliced

Tangy Sauce for Fish (page 226)

Preheat the oven to 450 degrees. Cut a large sheet of heavy-duty aluminum foil about 4 to 5 inches longer than the fish. Oil the dull side of the foil, and place the trout on the foil. Season both sides of the trout with salt, and open the fish out flat. Place the lemon slices, mint, parsley, and apple slices down the middle of the trout, and then fold the two sides together. Drizzle a little more oil over the fish. Fold up the foil, loosely folding the edges and then crimping them together tightly to make a packet. Place the packet on a baking sheet, and bake for about 15 minutes. To check for doneness, carefully open the packet, being mindful of the steam it will release. The flesh should be opaque and pull apart easily when tested with a fork. An instant-read digital thermometer should register 145 degrees. If the fish is not cooked through, close the packed and continue cooking another 3 to 5 minutes before rechecking.

Place the packet on a serving platter, and carefully cut across the top to open it, taking care not to let the steam from inside the packet burn you. Gently lift the fish out of the packet, and set it on a platter.

Starting with the top fillet, insert a sharp knife into the fish where the head and collar bone connect and slice through the skin and flesh to the bone. Cut along the natural division that runs down the spine until you reach the tail. Lift the fillet off the spine, and set it to the side. With your fingers, grab and lift the spine and the bone cage off the bottom fillet, leaving the bottom fillet behind. (The head usually comes off with the spine. Remove the cheeks to serve with the fillets.) Scrape out any membranes that cling to the fillets, and remove any remaining bones. Cut the fillets into portions. Serve the fish with the apple slices and a drizzle of your choice of sauce or vinaigrette (see headnote). Pass more sauce on the side.

Best Fried Fish

It's a thrill to see so many Native fisheries bringing culturally relevant fish back from the brink of extinction. On a visit to Northern Minnesota, I flash fried beautiful walleye from the Red Lake Nation Fishery, owned and operated by the Red Lake Band of Chippewa Indians. The same technique works beautifully with a range of light, white fillets, such as flounder, whitefish, cod, bass, and catfish.

The trick lies in the temperature of the oil and in the coating used on the fish. Use an oil with a high smoking point, such as bacon grease or lard. Canola, corn, peanut, avocado, and grapeseed oils also work well. Don't use butter or olive oil as they'll burn. The corn flour coating provides a delicious crispy texture and protects the fish from soaking up too much of the oil. A heavy-bottomed pan or a cast-iron skillet is best for distributing the heat evenly. Keep an eye on the skillet while frying. These go quickly! Don't forget to serve Hush Puppies (page 95) on the side.

Serves 4

½ cup corn flour

¼ teaspoon ancho chile powder

½ teaspoon salt

1 pound fish fillets

2 cups vegetable oil for frying

In a shallow bowl, stir together the flour, ancho chile powder, and salt. Dredge the fillets in the seasoned flour so they're thoroughly coated.

Pour the oil into a deep skillet, and set it over medium-high heat. When the oil begins to ripple and reaches 375 degrees on an instant-read thermometer, fry the fish in batches until it's crispy golden brown on both sides, about 6 minutes a side. Set the fish on a cooling rack to drain. Serve with Mom's Famous Chile Sauce (Piccalilli) (page 216) and Hush Puppies (page 95).

Hush Puppies

As long as you've got oil bubbling for frying fish, you may as well make the classic side—hush puppies.

Serves 4

1½ cups cornmeal

2 cups self-rising flour

¼ cup sugar

4 eggs

¼ cup milk

About one quart lard or vegetable oil for frying

In a large bowl, whisk together the cornmeal, flour, and sugar. In a small bowl, lightly beat the eggs with the milk. Stir the egg mixture into the cornmeal mixture to make a slightly stiff dough that pulls away from the side of the bowl. Add a little more flour if necessary.

In a large saucepan or deep-fat fryer, heat the oil until hot. Turn the heat to medium-low. Drop the batter by tablespoons into the oil, working in batches of 6 to 8 hush puppies at a time. Adjust the oil temperature as needed to keep it hot. Cook until the hush puppies puff up and turn themselves over, about 5 minutes. Remove the hush puppies with a slotted spoon, and drain them on paper towels. Set them in a low oven (200 degrees) to keep warm until ready to serve.

HOW TO EAT CRAWFISH

The crawfish meat is in the tail and it's easy to dig out:

- Hold the crawfish on either side of the tail joint. Your thumbs should be on one side of the shell, and your index fingers should be on the other side.

- Using a twisting motion, snap the head away from the tail.

- Using your thumbs, peel the shell away from the widest part of the tail as you would a shrimp.

- Holding the tail with one hand, tug out the tail meat with your other hand, then suck the head.

Mudbug Stew

Though crawfish are most often associated with the Southwest, Okies like me were raised on crawfish (mudbug) stew. The seasonings will vary from tribe to tribe and cook to cook, depending on who is stuffing the pot. The stew is great with a big plate of Blue Corn Biscuits (page 160).

Serves 4

3 tablespoons extra-virgin olive oil

1 large yellow onion, chopped

3 cloves garlic, smashed

1 small green bell pepper, seeded and chopped

1 stalk celery, chopped

3 pounds crawfish (see note)

1 (15-ounce) can diced tomatoes with their liquid

Generous pinch salt

Generous pinch cayenne

2 tablespoons filé powder

½ cup chopped green onions, plus more for garnish

¼ cup chopped cilantro, plus more for garnish

Heat the oil in a large heavy pot set over medium heat. Add the onion, garlic, bell pepper, and celery and cook, stirring, until the vegetables are soft and golden, about 10 to 12 minutes. Add the crawfish and cook, stirring occasionally, until they begin to throw off a little liquid, about 5 minutes.

Stir in the tomatoes and their liquid, salt, cayenne, filé powder, green onions, and cilantro. Simmer over medium-low heat until the crawfish have turned bright red and are cooked through, about 5 to 10 minutes. Serve garnished with more chopped green onions and cilantro.

Note: Crawfish are available frozen in most markets or online (see Sources, page 237). If using frozen, let the crawfish thaw for 10 minutes before adding them to the pot.

Shellfish Stock

This simple stock is great for just about any fish or shellfish soup or stew. It will keep about 2 days in the refrigerator in a covered container, and it freezes nicely.

Makes 2 to 3 cups

2 cups of shrimp, crab,
   or crawfish shells,
   or a mix of shells

½ cup white wine

1 small onion, quartered

1 small carrot

1 small bay leaf

Generous pinch salt

Put all of the ingredients into a large stock pot, and add enough water to cover them by 4 inches. Set the pot over medium-high heat, and bring the water to a slow boil. Reduce the heat, and simmer for 30 minutes. Pour the stock into a sieve set over a large bowl or pot and strain. Discard the contents of the sieve, and allow the stock to cool before transferring it to a covered container. Refrigerate or freeze the stock.

FOREST FLAVORS

Next time you simmer shellfish or braise a roast, try adding a bundle of pine needles or a small branch of cedar to the pot. Not too much, they're powerful. These forest flavors add notes of wood and a touch of spice to any pot. Just remember to remove them before serving. Be sure to avoid poisonous evergreens such as Norfolk Island pine and yew. Cedar, blue spruce, and juniper are good choices.

Mussels and Chanterelles Simmered with Pine Needles

There is no better way to cook mussels than by steaming them using the time-tried traditional method. It's simple: when the mussels cook, they release their flavorful juices so the liquid becomes a shellfish broth with an incredibly intense flavor. Add a handful of pine needles, a few wild mushrooms, and it's the taste of sea and forest in one pot. This recipe is the happy result of an afternoon foraging mussels along the Santa Cruz Coast with Chef Michel Nischan for one of our PBS episodes. On the forest path heading to the beach, we gathered the wild mushrooms and then picked up mussels as we hiked over tidal pools. We lit a fire, filled our pot with seawater, and simmered the mussels, mushrooms, and a small branch of pine. While this sounds wildly exotic, the method is easily replicated at home.

Serves 4 to 6

4 pounds mussels in shells

1 tablespoon extra-virgin olive oil

4 cloves garlic, smashed

Coarse salt

1 cup dry white wine or ocean water

1 small pine branch

½ pound chanterelle or shiitake mushrooms

Rinse the mussels under cold water. Remove any hairy clumps around the shells with a sharp knife or your fingers.

Heat the oil in a soup pot with a tight-fitting cover. Add the garlic and a pinch of salt, and sauté for about 3 minutes. Add the wine, a small pine branch, and the mushrooms, and bring the liquid to a simmer. Add the mussels and cover the pot. Steam the mussels, turning once, until they open, about 5 to 10 minutes. Use a slotted spoon to transfer the mushrooms and mussels to bowls, discarding the pine branch and any mussels that haven't opened. Taste, and adjust the seasoning.

GUMBO!

The Native Houma tribes in the Louisiana Bayou Region created the original filé gumbo. Filé is the finely ground leaves of indigenous sassafras used to both thicken and flavor the dish. The word *gumbo* refers to the okra brought from Africa by slaves. Natives taught the French Acadian people, who had been cast out of New Brunswick, Nova Scotia, and Prince Edward Island in the 1700s, the ways of the bayous and their cuisine. Indigenous gumbo is not thickened with a flour-based roux nor does it contain okra. Instead, this stew is thickened with the filé powder after it's simmered and rich. Be sure to avoid boiling the gumbo after the filé is added because it will become bitter.

Spicy Houma Shrimp

The Houma tribal communities are spread along the east side of the Red River of the South in Louisiana's Bayou Country. The Houma know the coastal waterways, and many earn a living fishing the region's shrimp and crawfish for their boldly seasoned seafood specialties. This is a dish I first made years ago for a Houma community celebration. Serve it over rice with a slab of Corn Dance Cornbread (page 153) and a side of potato salad (pages 54–55).

Serves 4 to 6

3 tablespoons extra-virgin olive oil

2 cloves garlic, minced

1 red bell pepper, seeded and chopped

1 yellow bell pepper, seeded and chopped

½ cup chopped yellow onion

2 pounds uncooked large shrimp, peeled and deveined

Salt

1 teaspoon Cajun seasoning (see note), or more to taste

½ cup dry white wine

Chopped parsley, for garnish

Juice of ½ lemon

Heat the oil in a large skillet. Add the garlic, peppers, and onion, and sauté until the vegetables are tender, about 5 minutes. Add the shrimp, and sprinkle them with salt and Cajun seasoning. Sauté until the shrimp begin turning pink, about 2 minutes. Add the wine to the skillet, and cook to reduce and intensify the flavors. Serve the shrimp garnished with the parsley and a generous dash of lemon.

Note: Use the Cajun seasoning blend you like best, or make your own by mixing 2½ teaspoons paprika, 2 teaspoons salt, 2 teaspoons garlic powder, 1¼ teaspoons dried oregano, 1¼ teaspoons dried thyme, 1 teaspoon onion powder, 1 teaspoon cayenne pepper, and ½ teaspoon red pepper flakes. Store in a covered jar.

Open Skies and Vast Prairies

WILD BIRDS, POULTRY, AND RABBIT

I learned to shoot ducks, geese, quail, and wild turkeys when Dad handed me a shotgun. I was about ten years old when I hoisted that gun against my shoulder and pulled the trigger. I can still feel the big kick that knocked me over. In the late fall, Dad and I would head out on those freezing-cold early mornings and hunker down in the duck blind, sip strong coffee, and wait as the decoys bobbed around on the semi-iced lake. Dad took pride in his hand-whittled duck calls that drew the birds overhead. To call wild turkeys, he'd take a washboard and rub it up and down with a rubber hose, replicating the sound of the turkey's gobble.

Achiote and Sassafras Marinated Quail

Bobwhite are large quail with delicious white breast meat; these birds are abundant in our area. They feast on acorns, pecans, and walnuts, so their meat is rich, nutty, and slightly sweet. The Gambel's quail, a different species, has meat that is dark and rich and closer to that of a duck.

If you're not a hunter, you can find quail in our markets that have been raised in captivity. You may have to ask the grocer to order them or find them online (see Sources, page 237). I've cooked quail my whole life, and I've found that the best way is to marinate them and then toss them on the grill or under the broiler. Our traditional Christmas breakfast is pan-fried quail with biscuits and gravy served with my Chile Cheese Casserole (page 76), and then the day is on.

These are tiny birds, so plan on serving one per person for an appetizer or two for a main dish. In this recipe, birch beer provides the sweet-woody notes of sassafras and the achiote paste adds a lovely kick.

Serves 4

¾ cup (5½ ounces) achiote paste

8 ounces birch beer or root beer

¼ cup cider or seasoned rice wine vinegar

1 teaspoon cumin seeds, toasted and ground (see note)

1 teaspoon coriander seeds, toasted and ground (see note)

1 tablespoon Mexican oregano

1 teaspoon salt

¼ cup honey

1 teaspoon smoke oil or liquid smoke

8 whole quail, preferably bobwhite

Crumble the achiote paste into a small bowl, then whisk in the birch beer, vinegar, cumin, coriander, oregano, salt, honey, and liquid smoke.

Cut along each side of the breastbone of each bird, then cut straight down along the ribs to where the thigh meets the body, to get two semi-boneless halves from each bird. (Don't worry if the skin holding the thigh and drumstick together separates.) Save the carcasses for stock. Put the quail and the achiote mixture in a nonreactive bowl or a heavy plastic bag, and stir or shake to coat. Marinate for at least an hour, or overnight.

Prepare a charcoal grill or set a gas grill or broiler to high. Grill or broil the quail, turning as needed, until it is browned and cooked through, about 15 minutes. To check for doneness, pull the thigh away from the breast: no red should be visible when poked with the tip of a sharp knife, and the juices should run clear. Serve hot or at room temperature.

Note: Toast the spices in a small, shallow skillet over medium heat, shaking the pan occasionally, until they become fragrant, about 30 seconds to 1 minute. Allow the spices to cool before grinding them in a spice mill or crushing them with a mortar and pestle.

Seared Duck Breast with Cranberry Pan Sauce

Duck breast and thighs are really two different meats. They are best cooked separately. A fat duck breast is no more difficult to cook than a steak; it's rich and dark and perfect with a tangy sauce such as the cranberry sauce or Rose Hip Sauce (page 229). It's quite lean, despite its fatty cap and skin, so cook it to a rosy medium-rare or it will turn tough and dry. If you're not a hunter (or aren't lucky enough to know a generous one), find Muscovy duck in butcher shops or online (see Sources, page 237).

Serves 4 to 6

DUCK

2 large duck breasts, about 1 pound each

Coarse salt

1 tablespoon grated fresh ginger

2 cloves garlic, minced

CRANBERRY SAUCE

1 shallot, finely diced

2 tablespoons balsamic vinegar

2 tablespoons maple syrup

6 ounces fresh cranberries

½ cup Turkey Stock (page 111) or chicken stock

Duck: Season both sides of the duck breasts with salt, then rub them with the ginger and garlic. Cover and marinate for 30 minutes at room temperature.

Place a heavy skillet or cast-iron pan over medium-high heat. When the pan is hot, lay the duck breasts in it skin-side down. Let the duck sizzle until the skin is crisp and golden, about 6 to 7 minutes. Turn the breasts over, and continue cooking until an instant-read thermometer reaches 125 degrees, about 3 to 5 minutes. Remove the duck from the pan, and let it rest for about 10 minutes on a warm plate. Drain the fat and save for another use.

Cranberry Sauce: Over medium heat, add the shallots to the pan you cooked the duck in and cook until they're softened, about 2 to 3 minutes. Add the vinegar, maple syrup, and most of the cranberries, stirring until the berries have popped. Stir in the stock, increase the heat, and bring to a boil to reduce the liquid until it's syrupy.

To serve, slice the duck breast thinly across the grain on a diagonal, and arrange the meat on a platter. Spoon the sauce over the meat, and garnish the duck with the remaining cranberries.

Duck or Turkey Stock

Duck or turkey stock is more flavorful than chicken stock, and it makes a wonderful base for soups and stews.

Makes about 2 quarts

4 pounds duck or turkey carcasses, meat removed

2 large onions, with skins, quartered

4 stalks celery, chopped

4 carrots, chopped

1 bay leaf

2 sprigs oregano

1 sprig sage

Preheat the oven to 350 degrees. Spread the carcasses on a baking sheet, and roast until they are nicely browned, about 10 to 15 minutes. Put the browned carcasses, onions, celery, carrots, bay leaf, oregano, and sage into a stockpot, and add enough water to cover the vegetables by 2 to 3 inches. Set the pot over high heat and bring the water to a boil, then reduce the heat and simmer for about 3 hours.

Set a cheesecloth-lined strainer over a large bowl. Use tongs to transfer and discard the bones from the stock. Pour the stock through the strainer into the bowl; discard the contents in the strainer. Allow the stock to cool to room temperature. Store the stock, refrigerated, in a covered container for up to a week, or freeze it.

Duck Confit with Fried Potatoes

Slow-roasting duck legs in the oven, uncovered, mimics the flavor and texture of real duck confit. This method takes far less time, yet produces tender meat with lovely crispy skin. Look for large duck legs, available at butcher shops and online (see Sources, page 237). I like to serve these duck legs with thinly sliced potatoes fried in the duck fat. Top with frizzled sage and a drizzle of Rose Hip Sauce (page 229) or Gingery Cranberry Jam (page 217) to bring the whole dish together.

Serves 4 to 6

4 to 6 large duck legs, about 12 ounces each, trimmed

Salt

1½ pounds Yukon Gold potatoes

Frizzled sage leaves, for garnish (see note on page 65)

Gingery Cranberry Jam (page 217) or Rose Hip Sauce (page 229)

Preheat the oven to 325 degrees. Season the duck legs generously with salt on both sides. Lay the duck legs on a cutting board, skin-side up. Use a skewer or the tip of a sharp knife to prick the skin of each leg all over.

Place the legs, skin-side up, in a single layer in a high-sided roasting pan. Roast, uncovered, until the meat is so tender it falls off the bone and the skin is very crisp, about 1½ to 2 hours. Remove the legs from the roasting pan. Allow the rendered fat to cool in the pan, then pour it into a jar and save it for frying the potatoes.

To prepare the potatoes, put them into a pot of generously salted water. Bring the water to a boil, and cook the potatoes until they are just tender but not falling apart. Drain the potatoes, and pat them dry. Cut them into ½-inch thick slices, and then quarter the slices.

Generously film a large skillet with reserved duck fat. Set the skillet over high heat. When it's hot, lay the potato slices in the skillet so they sizzle. When the bottom of the slices become golden brown, about 5 minutes, flip them and fry the other side. Remove and set aside.

Serve the duck on top of the potatoes, and garnish it with frizzled sage made with duck fat, and a drizzle of Rose Hip Sauce or Gingery Cranberry Jam.

Turkey Medallions with Cornbread-Sage Dressing and Cranberry-Piñon Sauce

This is one of our family's favorite recipes and a hit at Corn Dance Café. It's now a star on the menu at Thirty Nine Restaurant. Though it looks like a lot of steps, this dish comes together quickly.

Serves 4 to 6 (but is easily scaled back)

CORNBREAD-SAGE DRESSING

- 1 tablespoon extra-virgin olive oil
- 2 ribs celery, cut into ¼-inch dice
- 1 small yellow onion, cut into ¼-inch dice
- 2 teaspoons poultry seasoning
- 1 tablespoon chopped fresh sage
- 3½ to 4 cups Corn Dance Cornbread (page 153)
- ¼ to ½ cup Duck or Turkey Stock (page 111), or chicken stock

TURKEY MEDALLIONS

- 2 pounds turkey tenderloin, sliced into medallions and pounded to an even thickness
- ½ cup flour seasoned with salt
- 3 tablespoons extra-virgin olive oil

CRANBERRY-PIÑON SAUCE

- 1 cup Duck or Turkey Stock (page 111), or chicken stock
- ½ cup dry white wine
- 1 cup dried cranberries
- ¼ cup dried currants or small raisins
- 2 tablespoon toasted piñon nuts or toasted pecans, chopped
- Salt to taste

Cornbread-Sage Dressing: Preheat the oven to 325 degrees. Generously grease an 8 × 8 inch baking dish.

Film a large skillet with the oil, and set it over medium heat. Sauté the celery and onion until the vegetables are translucent, about 5 minutes. Stir in the poultry seasoning and the sage.

Put the crumbled cornbread into a bowl. Add the sautéed vegetables and just enough turkey stock to moisten the mixture. Turn the dressing into the baking dish. Bake until the dressing is cooked through and the top is golden, about 20 to 25 minutes.

Turkey: Dredge the turkey medallions in the seasoned flour. Film a large sauté pan with the oil and set it over medium-high heat. Working in batches so as not to crowd the pan, sizzle the turkey until golden, about 3 to 4 minutes per side. Remove the turkey, drain it on a paper towel–lined plate, and hold it in a warm oven until ready to serve.

Cranberry-Piñon Sauce: Drain off the oil from the sauté pan. Deglaze the pan with the stock, scraping up any brown bits sticking to the bottom of the pan. Add the wine, cranberries, and currants. Bring the sauce to a boil, then reduce the heat to a simmer and cook, stirring constantly, until the sauce is reduced by half, about 10 minutes. Adjust the seasonings, and stir in the piñons just before serving.

To serve, place ½ cup of the stuffing on a plate, and stack two to three turkey medallions on the dressing. Ladle the sauce over the turkey, and serve any remaining sauce on the side.

Whole Roast Goose with White and Sweet Potatoes

Goose is a bird that gives the cook a lot of beautiful fat for roasting potatoes, frying eggs, and crisping up cauliflower. Serve this with Gingery Cranberry Jam (page 217) or brassy Mom's Famous Chile Sauce (Piccalilli) (page 216). It's perfect for a crowd!

Serves 10 to 12

1 whole goose, about 12 pounds

Coarse salt

2 pounds red or Yukon Gold potatoes

1 pound sweet potatoes, cut into 2-inch chunks

Sprinkle the goose, inside and out, with the salt. Trim the wings and excess fat, and reserve them for another recipe.

Preheat the oven to 325 degrees. Using the tip of a sharp knife, lightly prick the top layer of the skin all over to allow the fat to run out as it roasts. (Be careful not to prick all the way into the meat). Place the goose on a rack in a deep roasting pan, and cook for 1 hour.

Put the white and the sweet potatoes into a big pot, and add enough water to cover them by 2 inches along with enough salt that the water tastes briny. Bring the water to a boil, then reduce the heat and simmer the potatoes until they are slightly tender but not cooked through, about 5 minutes. Drain the potatoes.

Remove the goose and drain off the fat, reserving it for another use. Add the potatoes and the sweet potatoes to the roasting pan, and return it to the oven. Continue roasting for another hour.

Reduce the oven temperature to 275 degrees, and continue roasting until an instant-read thermometer registers 165 degrees at the center of the breast, about another 30 to 45 minutes. Allow the bird to rest for about 20 minutes before carving. Serve the goose with the potatoes.

HOMINY

Hominy is ground from nixtamalized corn. Nixtamalizing is an ancient process of soaking field corn in an alkaline solution; the corn is then washed and hulled. Nixtamalization increases the corn's nutritional value, flavor, and aroma. It also helps make the niacin (vitamin B) content more available to the body, which helps prevent pellagra. Cornmeal ground from nixtamalized corn is the basis for tortillas.

Hominy and hominy grits (ground from nixtamalized corn) have a subtly sweet corn flavor and remain staples throughout Indigenous communities. Hominy is traditionally used in soups, stews, and casseroles.

Preparing dried hominy is like cooking dried beans: rinse and soak the kernels first, then simmer the corn until it's soft. Or look for canned hominy on the grocer's shelf; it's usually next to the canned beans.

Turkey Hominy Stew

This rich blend of turkey, hominy, and tomatoes is a wonderfully warming dish for late fall and winter, one that tastes even better a day or two after it's made. It freezes beautifully. Serve it with Loretta's Cornmeal Fry Bread (page 165).

Serves 6 to 8

2 tablespoons extra-virgin olive oil or duck fat

1 cup diced yellow onions

2 cloves garlic, minced

1 pound ground turkey

1 (10-ounce) can tomato sauce

1 (14.5-ounce) can diced tomatoes with their juice

1 cup Duck or Turkey Stock (page 111), or chicken stock

1 (15-ounce) can white hominy, drained

2 teaspoons crumbled dried Mexican oregano

1 tablespoon dark chili powder

1 teaspoon ground cumin

Salt

Generous pinch cayenne

Film a medium-sized stockpot with the oil, and set it over medium-high heat. Add the onions, and sauté until they're golden, about 3 to 5 minutes. Stir in the garlic, and cook until it is aromatic, about a minute. Stir in the turkey, breaking up the chunks with a spoon, and cook until it is browned and cooked through. Add the tomato sauce, tomatoes with their juices, stock, hominy, oregano, chili powder, and cumin. Add salt to taste. Bring the stew to a boil, then reduce the heat a little and simmer until the stew has thickened to the desired consistency. Season to taste with additional salt and cayenne.

PRAIRIE CHICKENS

Well before Europeans arrived, our prairies were filled with many different birds, and their songs filled the air. Prairie chickens are wild birds; their meat is closer to that of a grouse. Prairie chickens tend to be a little more tender than most other wild birds, with a dark flavor closer to duck. Unless you are a hunter or know one, dark chicken meat will suffice in the Potawatomi Chicken recipe.

Potawatomi Chicken

Here, everything roasts together—potatoes, chile and bell peppers, and lots of sage—for a weeknight one-pan meal. Top it off with watercress or arugula, and you've included salad as well. Serve this chicken for dinner tonight, and then pack the fixings onto a Little Big Pie (page 167) for lunch tomorrow.

Bone-in, skin-on chicken thighs, unlike the leaner breasts, tend to stay moist and are in less danger of overcooking. Make sure you spread everything out in one layer, essential for browning it all up.

Serves 4 to 6

1½ pounds bone-in, skin-on chicken thighs

1 pound small Yukon Gold potatoes, cut into ½-inch pieces

1 poblano or Anaheim chile, seeded and cut into 1-inch pieces

2 bell peppers, red and yellow, seeded and cut into 1-inch pieces

1 small onion, sliced ½-inch thick

Coarse salt

2 tablespoons thick hot sauce (such as harissa or Sriracha)

1 teaspoon ground cumin

2 tablespoons chopped fresh sage

3 to 4 tablespoons extra-virgin olive oil

Watercress or arugula

Balsamic vinegar

Heat the oven to 425 degrees. In a large bowl, toss together the chicken, potatoes, chile and bell peppers, and onion with a little salt. Toss in the hot sauce, cumin, sage, and enough oil to generously coat the chicken and vegetables. Spread the chicken and vegetables out on a baking sheet. Roast until everything is golden and cooked through, turning the chicken and vegetables occasionally, about 35 to 45 minutes.

Serve the chicken and vegetables together topped with handfuls of watercress and drizzled with a little of the rendered chicken fat and balsamic to taste.

Cornmeal-Dusted Rabbit

Rabbit, "the other white meat," is one of the most delicious and sustainable foods on the planet. As a kid, I loved the rabbit that Grandma Peltier dusted with cornmeal and sizzled off in bacon fat, then served with her tangy slaw. Her rabbit inspired this star item on the Corn Dance Café menu. Serve it with Jicama Slaw (page 45).

You can find rabbit at many local butcher shops and online (see Sources, page 237). With the growing interest in healthy, grass-fed meat, we are sure to find more rabbit in our stores soon.

The dry brine adds flavor to the meat without the fuss of soaking the rabbit in salt water or buttermilk. Serve the rabbit drizzled with Roasted Red Pepper Sauce (page 227) for a pretty presentation.

Serves 4

1 (3-pound) rabbit, cut into 6 pieces (save the rib cage for stock)

Coarse salt

1 garlic clove, crushed

½ teaspoon ground allspice

1 tablespoon whole-grain mustard

1 tablespoon chopped oregano

1 tablespoon chopped sage

1 cup red or yellow cornmeal, seasoned with salt

Vegetable oil for frying

Roasted Red Pepper Sauce (page 227)

Sprinkle the rabbit with salt. In a small bowl, mix the garlic, allspice, mustard, oregano, and sage. Rub the rabbit with the mixture, set the rabbit on a plate, cover it, and refrigerate overnight. If you're short on time, let the dry-brined rabbit stand, covered, for 30 minutes at room temperature.

Preheat the oven to 200 degrees. Dredge the rabbit pieces in the cornmeal. Pour about 3 inches of oil into a cast-iron skillet, and set it over medium-high heat. When the oil begins to ripple, add half the rabbit pieces and fry them until they're golden brown, about 8 to 10 minutes per side, and the thickest part of the rabbit registers 160 degrees on an instant-read thermometer. Transfer the fried rabbit to a wire rack placed on a baking sheet, and hold it in the warm oven until all the pieces are fried. Serve the rabbit drizzled with the Roasted Red Pepper Sauce.

On the Range and over the Plains

WILD GAME AND RANCH MEAT

Our family always had plenty of game—deer, elk, antelope—
and what we didn't grill or roast, we ground for burgers and
chili. The big game was processed in town and then stored
in the locker freezer, ready for everyday dinners as well
as family feasts. Working off memories of how my family
cooked game, I feature dishes of grilled, roasted, braised,
and pan-fried meat at Thirty Nine Restaurant.

I had learned to hunt with my Dad, and our sons took pride
in their abilities to ride and shoot, then dress and cook
what they'd bagged. Clay was a horseman, and Craig was
the cattleman, competing in 4-H shows.

Venison Shank Braised with Juniper and Sage

Whenever one of the hunters in our family brought home a deer, we cooked the shanks first. These form the most delicious cut—the meat and connective tissue melt into a rich sticky gravy. When properly braised, the dish feels as though it's silky with fat, but because venison is so lean, the process is alchemy. The key to cooking any shank, wild or not, is to use low, slow moist heat.

Serve these venison shanks with mashed potatoes or polenta to soak up the sauce. This recipe calls for what looks like a lot of garlic (2 full heads): no worries, the garlic mellows and melts into the sauce.

Serves 4 to 6

3 tablespoons extra-virgin olive oil

4 venison or lamb shanks

Salt

2 heads garlic, separated into cloves and peeled

1 cup chicken stock

1 cup red wine

1 tablespoon chopped sage

1 tablespoon juniper berries

Preheat the oven to 300 degrees. Season the shanks with a little salt. Film a Dutch oven with the oil, and brown the shanks well on all sides, about 15 minutes. Remove the shanks to a plate, and set it aside.

Add the garlic to the pot, and lightly brown it. Add the stock and wine, and scrape up any browned bits from the bottom of the pot with a wooden spoon. Increase the heat, add the sage and juniper berries, and bring the stock to a simmer. Return the shanks to the pot, arranging them shin-side up. Cover the pot, and put it in the oven. Cook until the meat begins to fall off the bone, about 2 hours.

Carefully remove the shanks, and arrange them on a baking sheet. Increase the oven heat to 400 degrees. Squeeze the garlic cloves into the braising liquid, and discard the skins.

Pour the braising liquid into a blender and puree it. Return the puree to the pot. Baste the shanks with the puree, and put the baking sheet in the oven. Roast, occasionally basting the shanks with the puree, until the shanks are nicely glazed, about 10 to 15 minutes. Serve the shanks on mashed potatoes or polenta, drizzled with more of the puree.

Grilled Elk Tenderloin

I love elk—it is fattier and less gamey tasting than deer, with a flavor that's closer to grass-fed beef. Each cut of the elk is different. The tenderloin is the most prized cut, tender, lightly sweet, and best when grilled.

Elk tenderloin medallions are perfect for the grill and just as delicious broiled; you want a little flame to kiss and char the meat to play up its sweetness. Elk medallions are a nice match to Sour Cherry Sauce (page 227) or Gingery Cranberry Jam (page 217).

Serves 4

8 elk loin medallions, about 3½ ounces each

3 tablespoons extra-virgin olive oil

Salt

Preheat the grill or the broiler to high. Brush the elk with the oil, and season it with salt. Grill or broil until the meat is just charred, about 3 minutes per side. Remove, and allow the meat to stand for about 3 to 5 minutes before serving it drizzled with Sour Cherry Sauce. Pass more sauce on the side.

Spice-Rubbed Bison Tenderloin Steaks

Bison tenderloin is very lean, so do not overcook it. When served rare or medium-rare, it's exquisitely tender, juicy, and lean with a deep and subtly sweet grassy flavor. In this recipe, the spices make a flavorful crust for this very tender cut. Serve it on a mound of Roasted-Garlic Mashed Potatoes (page 85).

Serves 4 to 6

1 whole chipotle pepper in adobo, seeded, or 1 teaspoon chipotle powder

½ teaspoon ground allspice

2 teaspoons red chili powder

2 teaspoons cumin seeds, toasted and ground (see note)

2 teaspoons coriander seeds, toasted and ground (see note)

¼ cup paprika

1 tablespoon maple sugar or brown sugar

1 tablespoon coarse salt

4 (8-ounce) bison tenderloin steaks

Heat a grill pan or warm the grill to medium-high. Combine the spices in a small bowl, and then turn the spice mixture onto a large flat plate. Dredge each steak in the spice mixture, shaking off the excess. Place the steak on the grill or grill pan. Lower the heat or move the steaks around so the spices don't burn. Grill about 4 to 5 minutes per side, then allow the steaks to rest for a couple of minutes before serving.

Note: Toast the spices in a small, shallow skillet over medium heat, shaking the pan occasionally, until they become fragrant, about 30 seconds to 1 minute. Allow to cool before grinding in a spice mill or crushing with a mortar and pestle.

BISON OR BUFFALO?

Although many people use the names interchangeably, bison and buffalo are different animals. Bison are found in North America and Europe; buffalo, such as water buffalo and Cape buffalo, are native to Africa and Asia.

Bison are also known as *tatanka* in Lakota, *bizhiki* in Ojibwe, and *pkoshuke* in Potawatomi. These majestic, powerful animals were once abundant across the American landscape, ranging from Canada to Mexico, New York to Oregon. At one time, before European contact, at least 30 million bison roamed the country. The Plains people followed the herds of bison that fed and sheltered them, providing blankets, knives, fuel, tipis, and tools—every part of the animal they hunted was put to very good use. Bison continue to play a key role in oral history, stories, and spiritual narratives.

The US government intentionally disrupted Native ways of life by killing off the bison, reducing the population of 30 million to about 325 by 1884. Many tribal communities have been on the forefront of bison conservation, developing herds on their lands to supply community members and school lunches with a delicious, nutritious source of protein. In addition, thanks to the collaborative efforts of tribal leaders and conservationists, over 20,000 bison now roam public lands.

These enormous animals—6½ feet tall and 2,000 pounds—are incredibly fast and agile, able to run up to 35 mph and leap an 8-foot fence in a single bound. They're confident and tough and well-adopted to the cold. Their shaggy winter coats are so thick that snow sits on top of them without touching their skin, and with their huge heads, they are able to plow snow out of their way to graze. Come spring, they shed their coats and frolic in the new grass and mud. The Intertribal Buffalo Council works with the National Parks to help protect bison and preserve bison traditions.

Braised Bison Short Ribs

Tender to the bone, these short ribs are finger-licking fabulous. They take a long time to cook; don't rush! If you can't find bison short ribs, beef ribs will work here too. This recipe is easily doubled or tripled; allow two short ribs per serving.

Do serve these short ribs with Roasted-Garlic Mashed Potatoes (page 85). They also make a terrific partner to any of the potato salads (pages 54–55).

Serves 4

8 bone-in bison short ribs, 1½ inches each

Salt

2 cups beef stock

2 cups red wine

1 tablespoon chopped sage

1 tablespoon grated lemon zest

¼ cup Loretta's Fierce Tomato Jam (page 219), or your favorite barbecue sauce

Preheat the oven to 275 degrees. Salt the short ribs on both sides, then lay them bone-side down in a baking dish, snuggling the ribs close together. Pour in the stock and wine. Sprinkle the sage and lemon zest on top, and cover the pan tightly with two sheets of aluminum foil.

Cook the ribs for at least 4 hours, or until the meat begins to separate from the bone and is extremely tender. Drain off any liquid or excess fat. Coat the ribs with the tomato jam, and return them to the oven to glaze, about 5 to 8 minutes.

Clay's Buffaloaf

This crowd-pleaser was created by my son Chef Clay for his Grand Boulevard Bar & Grill in Oklahoma City. The recipe swaps out ground beef for bison and quinoa for breadcrumbs as a gluten-free binder. It's lighter and spicier than most meatloaf, thanks to the chipotle and green chiles. It's a classic paired with Roasted-Garlic Mashed Potatoes (page 85). Next day, if you have any left, try slices on a Little Big Pie (page 167) with a side of Loretta's Quick Pickles (page 215).

Serves 6 to 8

½ cup quinoa

1½ pounds ground bison meat

¾ cup finely diced
    yellow onion

½ cup finely diced celery

½ cup finely diced carrots

2 eggs

2 tablespoons pureed
    canned chipotle peppers
    with adobo sauce

⅔ cup sugar- and salt-
    free tomato sauce

1 teaspoon ground sage

½ teaspoon cumin

1 pinch ground thyme

Salt

½ cup chopped green chiles

Preheat the oven to 350 degrees, and line a rimmed baking sheet with parchment.

Rinse the quinoa thoroughly. Bring 2 cups of water to a boil, and add the quinoa. Reduce the heat, cover, and simmer on medium-low until the quinoa's germ, or tail, appears, about 12 to 15 minutes. Remove the pot from the heat, drain any remaining water from the quinoa, and fluff it with a fork.

In a large bowl, gently mix the quinoa, bison, and other ingredients with your hands. Shape the mixture into a loaf, and gently place it on the baking sheet. Bake until the loaf is browned on the outside and cooked through, about 1 hour.

Jabo Burger

This recipe was created in honor of Dad (John Adams Barrett), who served as a frogman (predecessor to today's Navy SEALs) during WWII. Jabo was his nickname, Jabo the frogman. When I was a kid, our favorite lunch place served thin griddled burgers on a tender rye bun, slathered three times with a secret sauce—under the burger, on top of the burger, then on top of the tomato that topped the burger— with even more sauce passed alongside. It took me a while to create a recipe for the sauce based on taste memory. I keep some on hand for burgers and sandwiches.

Ground bison should be handled gently; too much mixing can make it tough. Cook these burgers to rare or medium-rare. The meat is very lean and will dry out quickly if overcooked. To retain their juices, sizzle the burgers in a cast-iron skillet or a heavy-duty frying pan, not on a grill. On a grill, the juices drip onto the flames causing them to flare, burning and drying out the meat.

Serves 6

JABO SAUCE

- 1 cup mayonnaise (preferably Hellman's)
- 1 to 2 tablespoons Thousand Island dressing
- 2 tablespoons finely chopped tomatoes
- ½ to 1 teaspoon pickled yellow chile peppers
- Several shots chile pepper brine

BURGERS

- 1½ to 2 pounds ground bison
- Coarse salt
- 2 tablespoons vegetable oil
- 6 soft rye buns
- 2 tomatoes, sliced thick

Jabo Sauce: In a small bowl, whisk together the mayonnaise, dressing, tomato, peppers, and chile pepper brine. Store any extra sauce in a covered container in the refrigerator for up to 4 days.

Burgers: Divide the meat into six even portions, and shape it into balls. One at a time, place a ball of meat between two pieces of parchment paper and gently press it between the backsides of two plates to form perfectly even burger patties. Season the patties with coarse salt.

Heat a cast-iron or heavy skillet over medium-high heat until it just begins to smoke. Add the oil and then the patties. Reduce the heat to medium. Cook until just browned on one side, flip, and cook until the burger is medium-rare, about 3 to 4 minutes per side.

To serve, slather the bottom of each bun with plenty of Jabo Sauce. Place a patty on each bun, then top with more sauce and a slice of tomato. Add more sauce on the tomato, and place the bun on top.

BISON JERKY

Dried bison, often called buffalo, is known as *wasna* in the Lakota language and *gazhakdek* in my Potawatomi (Anishinaabe) (literally, "dried meat").

In Lakota, *wa* means "anything" and *sna* means "ground up." Wasna is a mix of dried meat or corn and dried berries pounded together and bound with fat. Think of jerky, a salty-sweet, dried fruit snack. This is different from my Nation's version.

I learned to make wasna on the Cheyenne River Sioux reservation from the lovely Jeri while taping *Seasoned with Spirit*. I loved the way we made dried chokecherry patties from the freshly picked fruit as well as how she cut and hung the meat from a rack made of sticks and limbs from the surrounding trees. Together, using a pounding stone, we ground and pounded the dried fruit and meat together in a beautiful hard-leather bowl while adding the crystal-clear kidney fat from the bison. This was one of the most rewarding food experiences I've had.

Since I was a child, I have loved, loved, loved mincemeat pie when the holidays rolled around, and in my mind, these various meat and fruit preparations are the early versions of my beloved mincemeat pie!

This traditional method of preservation provided pantry staples that nourished tribal communities through harsh winters. Wasna contains equal amounts of dried berries and dried meat or corn, pounded together. It packs a nutritional punch.

I make wasna to garnish salads, soups, and stews. It is a simple process of cutting the meat into very thin strips and then dehydrating the meat and the berries in a very low oven. Once the ingredients are very dry, I pound them together with a little fat. Bison fat is the best; rendered from the kidneys, it's crystal clear and very clean tasting.

Barbecue Bison Brisket

When I'm invited to cook at different tribal events, I'm often gifted a big cut of meat—bison, elk, venison, or antelope. This sure-fire recipe always satisfies. Thanks to the low heat and long roasting time, the meat becomes fork tender and succulent. It's perfect for a feast, and leftovers are especially delicious in a Little Big Pie (page 167). Pair the brisket with Corn Dance Cornbread (page 153).

Serves 12

1 (6- to 7-pound) bison brisket

Garlic powder

Onion powder

Celery salt

2 tablespoons liquid smoke

1 (10-ounce) bottle Worcestershire sauce

10 ounces water

Hickory barbecue sauce

Preheat the oven to 250 degrees. Generously coat the brisket with garlic powder, onion powder, and celery salt. Put the brisket into a baking dish, and add the liquid smoke, Worcestershire sauce, and an equal amount of water. Cover the dish tightly with aluminum foil, and bake until the meat falls apart when pulled with a fork, 6 to 8 hours.

Remove the brisket, and set it on a carving board. Turn half of the cooking liquid into a saucepan, and add an equal amount of barbecue sauce. Set the pan over low heat to simmer, and reduce slightly, about 5 minutes.

Trim the fat from the brisket. Cut the brisket across the grain into thick slices and then into chunks. Return the brisket to the baking dish, and cover it with the sauce. Return to the oven to warm, if necessary. Serve the brisket with the sauce.

Hearty Bison Stew

The heady scents of this stew burbling away will draw everyone into the kitchen. Serve it over grits or mashed potatoes and with a side of Corn Dance Cornbread (page 153). Leftovers are great in Little Big Pies (page 167).

Serves 6

2 tablespoons extra-virgin olive oil

2 pounds bison meat, cut into 1-inch cubes

1 cup diced white onion

1 cup diced carrots

1 cup diced celery

4 cloves garlic, diced

½ cup tomato paste

4 cups Dark Stock (page 143) or beef stock

4 cups red wine

1 (14.5-ounce) can chopped tomatoes with their juice

10 to 12 juniper berries, crushed

Salt

Generous pinch ancho chile powder

1 tablespoon chopped sage

Film a large saucepan with the oil, and set it over medium-high heat. Brown the bison on all sides until golden brown, then remove it to a platter with a slotted spoon.

In the same pan, add the onion, carrots, celery, garlic, and tomato paste. Slowly add the stock, wine, and tomatoes. Season with salt, ancho chile powder, and sage. Return the meat to the pan, reduce the heat, and simmer until the liquid is reduced by half, about 45 minutes. The meat should be fork tender.

STOCKING UP

Mom always seemed to have a stockpot simmering away on the back of the stove. It was repeatedly replenished with the bones and vegetable scraps from whatever she happened to be cooking. Nothing went to waste.

These days, given our hurly-burly schedules, making stock is often the last thing on a cook's list of things to do. A number of great-quality boxed stocks are available. Look for low-sodium or salt-free prepared stocks made with organic ingredients. Pacific is my choice for stock and bone broth.

Dark Stock (Bison, Lamb, Venison)

There's no doubt that your own homemade stock is tastier and healthier than any you can buy in a box. For this simple recipe, use whatever leftover bones you happen to have on hand—bison, lamb, venison, elk, or beef.

Makes about 2 quarts

About 4 pounds bones

1 carrot, cut into
  2-inch pieces

1 large skin-on onion,
  quartered

1 small fennel bulb

Several sprigs parsley

1 sprig sage

1 leek, white part only,
  split, rinsed, and cut
  into 2-inch pieces

1 tablespoon tomato paste

Preheat the oven to 350 degrees. Put the bones onto a baking sheet, and roast the bones until they are nicely browned, about 15 minutes.

Put all of the ingredients into a stockpot, and add enough water to cover them by about 1 inch. Set the pot over high heat, and bring the water to a boil. Reduce the heat to low, skim off any impurities that rise to the surface, and simmer, partially covered, for about 6 to 8 hours.

Strain the stock into another pot through a sieve lined with a double layer of cheesecloth. Discard the contents of the sieve. Allow the stock to cool to room temperature, and skim it again. Store the stock in the refrigerator for up to 4 days, or freeze for up to 3 months.

Loretta's Chili

This dish is on every one of my menus and is billed as "Kick-Ass Buffalo Chili" for its spicy, smoky heat. The ladies who came into Corn Dance for lunch would giggle whenever they ordered it, often pointing to the menu instead of saying the name out loud.

Legend has it that chili traces its roots to the Old West of the nineteenth century, when cowboy cooks sizzled off boldly seasoned stews of thick chunks of meat, simmered in a kettle set over the open fire.

Serve the chili topped with plenty of chopped cilantro and a side of Loretta's Cornmeal Fry Bread (page 165). Leftovers are great served in a Little Big Pie Dough Bowl (page 168).

Serves 6 to 8

2 pounds bison roast, cut into 1-inch chunks

Salt

2 tablespoons corn or sunflower oil

1 large yellow onion, chopped

3 cloves garlic, smashed

1 green bell pepper, seeded and cut into ½-inch dice

1 red bell pepper, seeded and cut into ½-inch dice

1 to 2 tablespoons chili powder

2 teaspoons ground cumin

Generous pinch cayenne

1 (28-ounce) can diced tomatoes with their juice

1 to 2 cups Dark Stock (page 143) or beef broth

Season the meat with salt. Film a large Dutch oven or saucepan with the oil, and set it over medium-high heat. Sear the meat until it's browned all over, then stir in the onions and garlic and cook until the onions are limp and beginning to brown. Stir in the bell peppers, cover the pan, and cook until the bell peppers release their juices, about 3 minutes. Stir in the chili powder, cumin, and cayenne, and cook until the spices smell fragrant, about 1 to 2 minutes. Stir in the tomatoes with their juices and the stock. Simmer, stirring the pot occasionally, until the liquid is thick and the seasonings have come together, about 45 minutes to an hour. Taste, and adjust the seasonings.

Pan-Roasted Herb-Crusted Lamb Chops

This recipe calls for Navajo-Churro lamb. Its meat is sweet in flavor compared with commercial breeds. Because the animals range free along the high plains, they are lean, healthy, and taste of the wild sage they feast upon. You can find this heritage meat in some butcher shops or online (see Sources, page 237). Commercial lamb will work well in this recipe too. Serve the lamb chops with a generous dollop of Pineapple Serrano Salsa (page 233).

Serves 4

4 cloves garlic, smashed

1 tablespoon fresh thyme leaves, lightly crushed

1 tablespoon fresh oregano leaves, lightly crushed

2 teaspoons coarse salt

2 tablespoons extra-virgin olive oil

6 (1¼-inch-thick) lamb loin chops

In a small bowl, stir together the garlic, thyme, oregano, salt, and just enough of the olive oil (about 2 teaspoons) to make a paste. Smear this paste over the lamb chops.

Preheat the oven to 400 degrees. Film a heavy, ovenproof skillet with the remaining oil, and set it over high heat. Add the lamb chops, and cook them until they're until browned, about 3 minutes per side. Transfer the skillet to the oven, and roast the lamb chops about 10 minutes for medium-rare. Transfer the lamb to a platter, cover it, and let the lamb rest for 5 minutes.

Lamb-Stuffed Bell Peppers

These pretty stuffed peppers make a wonderful weeknight dinner. Feel free to sub in ground bison or turkey for the lamb, depending on what you have at hand.

Serves 6

6 bell peppers, a mix of green, red, orange, and yellow

1 pound ground lamb

½ pound mushrooms, chopped

2 cups cooked wild rice (see Wild Rice, page 38)

2 onions, coarsely chopped

1 zucchini, cut into ¼-inch cubes

2 tablespoons tomato paste

½ teaspoon coarse salt

½ teaspoon ancho chile powder

1½ tablespoons extra-virgin olive oil

Preheat the oven to 350 degrees. Cut around the stem ends of the peppers and remove the "hat" from each. Trim the hats at the base so they are about ½ inch thick, and set them aside. Remove and discard the seeds, and trim out the peppers' veins. Stand the peppers upright side by side in a gratin dish.

In a bowl, stir together the ground lamb, mushrooms, wild rice, onions, zucchini, tomato paste, salt, and ancho chile powder, and mix well. Stuff the peppers with this mixture, and place the hats on top.

Drizzle olive oil over the peppers, then add about 1 cup of water to the pan. Bake for 1 hour, 15 minutes. Serve basted with the pan juices.

Loretta's Big Biscuits with Sausage Gravy

I was the proud mom of my 4-H son, Craig, and in charge of breakfast for our early trials in the cattle barn. We served this sausage gravy on big home-baked biscuits. It is plenty hearty and kept us going through lunch. Venison is so very lean that it needs a little ground pork to keep it moist while it sizzles.

Yields 3 pounds of bulk sausage, serves about 6 to 8

2 pounds ground venison

1 pound ground pork

1 teaspoon coarse salt

½ teaspoon crushed red pepper flakes

1 teaspoon dried sage

2 tablespoons extra-virgin olive oil

2 tablespoons all-purpose flour

1 to 2 cups whole milk

6 to 8 Grandma Peltier's Biscuits (page 157)

Put the venison and pork into a large bowl and add the salt, crushed red pepper, and sage and mix well. To taste for seasoning, cook a small piece in an oil-slicked skillet over medium heat. (You don't want to taste it raw.) Adjust the seasoning.

Film a large skillet with the oil, and set it over medium heat. Add the sausage meat and cook, breaking up the pieces, until it's no longer pink, about 4 to 5 minutes. Whisk in the flour, and stir frequently until the mixture is barely tan, about 1 to 2 minutes. Slowly whisk in the milk, and keep stirring until the liquid thickens, about 8 to 10 minutes. Season with salt to taste. Serve the sausage gravy over the biscuits.

Fresh Baked

CORNBREAD, BISCUITS, AND LITTLE BIG PIES

I come from a long line of baking women who just seemed to have a feel for how much butter or bacon grease to add to biscuit dough and sensed exactly when to take the cornbread out of the oven. They seldom measured and never used an oven timer—they just knew. As a young girl, I was lucky enough to stand on a chair turned backward to the counter to help cut biscuits with a Welch's Grape Jelly glass, to spoon cornbread batter into the corn cob–shaped cast-iron baking pan that I still use today.

As I've traveled through the country, I've been graced with stories and recipes from elders who are working to return our heritage varieties of field corn to our gardens and kitchens. These recipes, and their stories, are meant to share.

Corn Dance Cornbread

As soon as I see the Shawnee Milling Company billboard at the Shawnee city limits, I know I am home. This is the recipe printed on every bag of Shawnee Best Yellow Corn Meal. It's the recipe my Grandmothers and Mother relied on for tender, slightly sweet, and moist cornbread. They used the rendered bacon fat they kept in a coffee can under the sink. Try it! It adds flavor and texture to the resulting loaf. This cornbread is the basis for Cornbread-Sage Dressing (page 114).

Makes an 8-inch round or square loaf, 6 corn sticks, or 6 small muffins

1 cup organic, stone-ground yellow cornmeal

1 cup all-purpose flour

1 teaspoon baking powder

1 teaspoon salt

1 egg, beaten

1 cup skim milk

2 tablespoons canola oil or bacon fat

1 cup fresh corn kernels, roasted (see note)

Preheat the oven to 325 degrees and generously grease an 8 × 8 inch baking pan, a corn-stick mold, 6 small cast-iron skillets, or an 8-inch cast-iron skillet.

In a large bowl, stir together the cornmeal, flour, baking powder, and salt. Stir in the egg, milk, and oil. Fold in the corn kernels. Pour the batter into the prepared pan, and bake until a toothpick inserted in the center comes up clean, about 25 to 30 minutes. (Allow 10 to 15 minutes for a corn-stick mold; 15 to 20 minutes for rounds baked in small skillets.)

Note: To roast corn kernels, film a skillet with a little oil, and set it over medium-high heat. Add the corn kernels, and sauté until they're nicely browned, about 5 to 10 minutes. Remove and cool before adding the roasted corn to the batter. You can also grill a whole ear of corn over an open fire until it's lightly toasted. Remove the corn and, when cool, cut the kernels from the cob.

Spicy cornbread variation: To spice things up, add 1 seeded, chopped jalapeño and one seeded, chopped green bell pepper along with the corn kernels.

Dr. John Mohawk's Hot Water Cornbread

Iroquois White Corn Project's roasted white corn flour and white corn flour make fabulous cornbread. The roasted white corn flour has a toasty essence, while the white corn flour is delicately sweet. Try them both; they mix and match splendidly. This recipe was developed by Dr. John Mohawk to showcase the corn's unique flavor. It's best baked in a springform pan to produce a loaf that resembles traditional cornbread.

Makes a 6-inch round loaf

2 tablespoons olive oil

2 cups boiling water

Generous pinch salt

2 cups Iroquois white corn flour

Preheat the oven to 325 degrees. Oil a 6-inch springform pan or baking dish.

Put the water into a medium bowl. Stir in the salt and the corn flour until it's absorbed, adding more water as needed. Pour the batter into the pan, and smooth the batter with a little cold water. Cover the pan with aluminum foil and bake for 1 hour. Remove from the oven and allow to cool, then refrigerate until cold. To serve, steam, grill, or sizzle slices of cornbread in a skillet filmed with fat or butter.

Variations: For a sweeter version, stir dried fruit and maple syrup or honey into the batter before baking. For savory versions, stir toasted pine nuts, caramelized onions, or chopped fresh sage or oregano—or a mixture of these ingredients—into the batter before baking.

GANONDAGAN IROQUOIS WHITE CORN

Iroquois white corn is an heirloom variety of field corn that dates back at least 2,000 years in the Haudenosaunee community. It is tender with a distinctly nutty, corny flavor. The Iroquois White Corn Project is the vision of Dr. John Mohawk (Seneca) and Dr. Yvonne Dion-Buffalo (Samson Cree). They devoted much of their careers to bringing Iroquois white corn back to the homes of the Haudenosaunee (Iroquois) people by engaging tribal farmers to grow it for everyday use. The project was picked up by my wonderful Seneca friends Jeanette Miller Jemison and Peter Jemison and is now a program of the Friends of Ganondagan, in Victor, New York. I had the great honor of working with John and Yvonne numerous times; he shared his cornbread recipe with me. Iroquois white corn is non-GMO, has a low glycemic index, and is less sweet and far more nutritious than contemporary varieties of corn. Products made from it are 100 percent natural (see Sources, page 237).

Johnny Cakes

There's a debate about how these simple corn pancakes got their name. It could be they were once called "journey cakes," because they could be packed up and taken out on the trail. The recipe calls for few ingredients and can be made sweet or savory.

Serves 4 to 6

2½ cups cornmeal

1 teaspoon salt

2½ cups boiling water

2 teaspoons maple syrup or honey

Bacon fat or oil

In a large bowl, stir together the cornmeal and salt. Slowly add the water and then the maple syrup, and stir until just combined; do not overmix. Heat a griddle or large skillet or frying pan over medium heat. The griddle is ready when drops of water sprinkled on it dance across the top. Spread a little of the fat over the surface. Place about ¼ cup of batter on the griddle. Once the edges dry and bubbles rise to the surface, about 30 seconds, flip the cake over with a wide spatula and cook through.

Grandma Peltier's Biscuits

Grandma Peltier mastered a lot of tasks in her life: she was known for her garden, her award-winning jellies and preserves, and her tender, fluffy biscuits. She made the clothes for her nine children. After she finished up a bag of commodity flour making these biscuits, she turned the flour sack into a tea towel or an apron. Grandma Peltier never learned to drive a car, she never followed a recipe, and she knew every star in the sky along with the legends of each constellation.

The less you touch or work the dough, the lighter and more tender the biscuits. You can use a Welch's Grape Jelly jar to cut the biscuits into 2-inch rounds. Use a 4-inch biscuit cutter to make bigger biscuits for Loretta's Big Biscuits with Sausage Gravy (page 147).

Makes eighteen 2-inch biscuits

Bacon fat to grease the pan

2 cups all-purpose flour (preferably Shawnee Best)

4 teaspoons baking powder

1 teaspoon salt

3 tablespoons good lard

¾ to 1 cup milk

Preheat the oven to 450 degrees. Line a baking sheet with parchment paper or lightly grease it with bacon fat.

In a large bowl, stir together the flour, baking powder, and salt. Using a pastry cutter or your fingertips, cut in the lard until the mixture resembles coarse crumbs. Add the milk and lightly mix to make a soft dough. Turn the dough onto a lightly floured surface, and lightly knead it with floured hands. Roll out the dough to a half-inch thickness. Cut rounds using a biscuit cutter, jelly jar, or juice glass, and place them on the baking sheet. Bake until golden, about 10 to 12 minutes.

Pumpkin Cream Biscuits

Pumpkin makes for a dense, soft biscuit, the perfect partner to breakfast eggs or a cup of afternoon coffee. Drizzle these biscuits with honey or slather them with Sage Butter (page 169) or Sand Plum Jelly (page 221).

Makes about eighteen 2-inch biscuits

2 cups all-purpose flour

4 teaspoons baking powder

1 teaspoon salt

1 teaspoon ground allspice

1 cup heavy cream

½ cup pumpkin puree

Preheat the oven to 400 degrees. Line a baking sheet with parchment paper or lightly grease it with oil.

In a small bowl, mix the flour, baking powder, salt, and allspice. In a large mixing bowl, whisk together the cream and the pumpkin puree. Turn the wet ingredients into the dry ingredients, and stir until a cohesive dough forms.

Transfer the dough onto a lightly floured surface, and lightly knead with floured hands. Roll out the dough to a half-inch thickness. Cut rounds using a biscuit cutter, jelly jar, or juice glass, and place them on the baking sheet. Bake until golden, about 10 to 12 minutes.

Blue Corn Biscuits

Deep and rich, blue cornmeal adds flavor, color, and texture to any recipe calling for cornmeal. Many Native tribes grow and grind their variety of blue field corn. I favor the blue cornmeal from the Ute Mountain Ute Tribe Farm & Ranch Enterprise (see Sources, page 237).

In this recipe, the blue cornmeal gives these biscuits a lovely crunch and blueish hue. If you prefer, sub out the blue cornmeal for yellow to create golden biscuits. Lightly sweet with a slight buttermilk tang, these biscuits are just right for shortcakes loaded with fresh berries or to accompany Butternut Squash Soup with Frizzled Sage and Toasted Squash Seeds (page 65). Top them with Loretta's Fierce Tomato Jam (page 219).

Makes about twelve 2-inch biscuits

1½ cups all-purpose flour

½ cup blue cornmeal

2½ teaspoons baking powder

½ teaspoon salt

⅓ cup vegetable shortening

¾ cup buttermilk, or

¾ cup milk with 1 tablespoon vinegar

Preheat the oven to 425 degrees. Line a baking sheet with parchment or lightly grease it.

In a large bowl, stir together the flour, cornmeal, baking powder, and salt. With a pastry cutter or your fingers, work the shortening into the flour to make a mixture that resembles crumbs. Stir in the buttermilk until the ingredients are just moistened.

Transfer the dough onto a lightly floured surface, and lightly knead it with floured hands. Roll out the dough to a half-inch thickness. Cut rounds using a biscuit cutter, jelly jar, or juice glass, and place them on the baking sheets. Bake until golden, about 10 to 12 minutes.

COFFEE CAN BREAD

My Grandma Peltier didn't own fancy loaf pans, so she baked her tea breads in coffee cans. The rounds were sliced into perfect half-moons that looked lovely topped with her homemade jams. Sweet breads make a wonderful gift.

Spicy Sweet Potato Bread

This orange beauty is incredibly moist and fragrant; slice it into pretty wheels or half-moons and serve it with Hibiscus Butter (page 169) or Sand Plum Jelly (page 221). Substitute sweet squash or pumpkin for the sweet potato puree.

Makes a 6-inch round or a 9 × 5 inch loaf

1¾ cups all-purpose flour

1 teaspoon baking powder

2 teaspoons ground cinnamon

½ teaspoon ground allspice

¼ teaspoon ground ginger

¾ teaspoon salt

2 eggs

1 cup maple sugar or brown sugar

1½ cups sweet potato puree

½ cup vegetable oil

¼ cup cranberry juice

½ cup toasted walnuts, pecans, or both, chopped

½ cup dried cranberries

Preheat the oven to 350 degrees. Generously grease and lightly flour a coffee can or a 9 × 5 inch loaf pan.

In a large bowl, whisk together the flour, baking powder, cinnamon, allspice, ginger, and salt. In a medium bowl whisk together the eggs and sugar, then whisk in the sweet potato puree, oil, and cranberry juice. Pour the wet ingredients into the dry, and gently mix them with a rubber spatula or a wooden spoon. Do not overmix. Stir in the nuts and cranberries.

Pour the batter into the prepared pan. If using a coffee can, lightly cover the top with aluminum foil and set it on a baking sheet. The bread is done when a toothpick inserted in the center comes out clean, about 60 to 65 minutes.

Allow the bread to cool completely in the pan before removing it. If the bread in the coffee can seems stuck, open the bottom of the can with a can opener and gently push the loaf out.

Persimmon Bread

Persimmons grow wild in Oklahoma, and in texture and taste seem like a cross between a pumpkin and an apple. While they're fabulous eating out of hand, they make wonderful tea breads, muffins, and puddings. Make this bread when the persimmons are very ripe and super soft. If you can't find persimmons, substitute 1 cup of canned or pureed pumpkin. Loaded with vitamin C, persimmons are extremely nutritious.

Makes one 9 × 5 inch loaf

½ cup raisins

¾ cup all-purpose flour, plus more for the pan

¾ cup whole wheat flour

1 teaspoon baking soda

1 teaspoon coarse salt

1 teaspoon ground cinnamon

4 large persimmons

⅓ cup buttermilk

2 tablespoons grated orange zest

½ cup (1 stick) unsalted butter, plus more for the pan

1 cup sugar

2 eggs

Preheat the oven to 350 degrees. Butter and flour a 9 × 5 inch loaf pan. Tap out any excess flour.

In a small bowl, stir together the raisins and 2 tablespoons hot water in a heatproof bowl. Let the raisins steep till they're plump, about 10 minutes.

In a medium bowl, whisk together the ¾ cup all-purpose flour, whole wheat flour, baking soda, salt, and cinnamon.

Scoop the persimmon flesh out with a spoon, turn it into a blender, and puree until it's smooth. Transfer 1 cup of the puree into another medium bowl, and whisk in the buttermilk and orange zest.

Using an electric mixer, beat the ½ cup of butter in a medium bowl until light and creamy, about 2 minutes. Add the sugar, and beat until light and fluffy, 3 to 4 minutes. Beat in the eggs one at a time until well mixed. Gradually add the persimmon mixture; beat well until combined. Add the dry ingredients in 3 batches, beating until just incorporated. Fold in the strained raisins. Pour the batter into the prepared loaf pan, and bake until a tester inserted into its center comes up clean, about 1 hour. Let the bread cool in the pan for 20 minutes. Unmold the bread, and let it cool completely on a wire rack.

Loretta's Cornmeal Fry Bread

Think of Indian food, and fry bread is often the first thing that comes to mind. But fry bread is *not* Indigenous, and it certainly isn't traditional. Its origins trace back to the internment camps that arose from the forced displacement of tribes in the mid-1800s. A plate-sized disk of lard-fried white-flour dough is, in fact, delicious; yet its history is brutal, an example of profit over a people's health. Like southern hushpuppies or Irish corned beef, foods that also wreak havoc on the arteries, fry bread is a food of survival and resilience.

The shape, taste, and color of fry bread varies by region, family, and tribe. This version is a hybrid of my family's hush puppies and the fry breads I've eaten in my travels to tribes across the United States. Made with cornmeal, this fry bread is sweeter and denser than most. It's great with Turkey Hominy Stew (page 118) or Loretta's Chili (page 144).

Makes about 16 to 20 fry bread

1½ cup finely ground cornmeal

½ cup all-purpose flour

1½ teaspoon salt

1½ teaspoon baking soda

1 large egg

1 cup buttermilk

Vegetable oil for frying, about 4 cups

Cover a large plate with a double layer of paper towels. In a large bowl, whisk together the cornmeal, flour, salt, and baking soda. In a smaller bowl, whisk together the egg and buttermilk. Stir the dry ingredients into the wet ingredients until they're just combined.

Fill a Dutch oven with 1½ inches of oil, and set it over medium-high heat until the oil begins to ripple and reaches about 365 degrees on an instant-read thermometer. Use an ice cream scoop or a serving spoon to portion the dough, then shape each portion into a relatively flat, oblong disk. Working in batches, fry the bread, turning it frequently with tongs until browned on all sides, about 3 to 4 minutes. Transfer the fry bread to the paper towel–lined plate to drain. Serve hot.

LITTLE BIG PIES

Little Big Pies are easier to make, tastier, and certainly healthier than fry bread. Baked, not fried, they make wonderful use of leftover braised meats and vegetables. Form them over a bowl for a wonderful container for salads, soups, stews, and chilies. Here are some ideas to get you started.

LITTLE BIG PIE HOT AND TASTY OPTIONS

Arrange a layer of these toppings on top of the unbaked dough, and bake for about 8 to 10 minutes:

Clay's Buffaloaf (page 136)
Barbecue Bison Brisket (page 140)
Mudbug Stew (page 98)
Spicy Houma Shrimp (page 105)
Loretta's Chili (page 144)
Turkey Medallions and Cranberry-Piñon Sauce (page 114)
Potawatomi Chicken (page 120)

LITTLE BIG PIE SALAD OPTIONS

These crusts, once baked, are wonderful topped with salads and roasted vegetables. Prepare the dough rounds and bake, untopped, until nicely browned, about 8 to 10 minutes. Remove, cool, then top with one of the following:

Nopales and Fiery Mango Salad with Chipotle Vinaigrette (page 42)
Sunchoke, Jicama, Avocado, and Pineapple Salad with Spicy Vinaigrette (page 51)
Three Sisters and Friends Salad (page 36)

Photo by Kitty Leaken

Little Big Pie Dough

This is the basic Little Big Pie dough recipe. It's great topped with Clay's Buffaloaf (page 136) or any grilled or braised meat, then baked off into individual open-face hand pies. You can make the dough in advance and hold it in the refrigerator until you're ready to bake.

Makes six 9-inch Little Big Pies

2¾ cups bread flour

1 teaspoon salt

1 teaspoon active dry yeast

½ teaspoon sugar

¾ cup warm (110 degrees) water

1 tablespoon extra-virgin olive oil, plus more for brushing the dough

Sift the flour and salt into a medium bowl. In a small bowl, whisk together the yeast, sugar, and ¼ cup of the warm water: let the yeast proof until it's frothy. Pour the yeast water into the flour along with the remaining warm water and olive oil. Mix the dough until it's soft. Turn the dough out onto a lightly floured surface, and knead with floured hands until it's elastic and firm (the texture of your earlobe or a baby's bottom).

Place the dough into a greased bowl, cover the bowl with plastic wrap, and set it in a warm place to rise until the dough has doubled in size, about 45 minutes. Punch the dough down, and knead it lightly.

Preheat the oven to 500 degrees. Line two baking sheets with parchment paper. Put the dough onto a lightly floured board or countertop, and cut it into six pieces. Pat the pieces into 6-inch rounds, and place them on the baking sheets. Brush each dough round with olive oil, and poke holes into the dough with a fork. Spoon a 2-inch layer of toppings onto the dough, and spread it evenly across the dough's surface.

Place the baking sheets into the oven, and bake until the crust is nicely browned and the topping is bubbly, about 8 to 10 minutes.

Cornmeal variation: Reduce the amount of flour to 2¼ cups, and add ⅓ cup of cornmeal.

Little Big Pie Dough Bowls: Turn six soup or metal mixing bowls upside down on a baking sheet, and lightly grease them. Drape the flattened dough over the bowls, and bake in a 500-degree oven until the bread is golden and firm. Allow the bread bowls to cool before lifting them off the soup bowls.

SEASONED BUTTER

At Corn Dance Café, we served these seasoned butters alongside bread baskets filled with our biscuits (page 157) and corn sticks (pages 153 and 154). They take just a minute to prepare. Present the butter in small dishes, or shape the butter into logs, wrap them in parchment paper, and refrigerate them till they're firm enough to slice. Store the butter in the refrigerator, or freeze it.

Sage Butter: In a small bowl, smash 1 tablespoon of chopped fresh sage and a pinch of salt into 1 stick (½ cup) of softened unsalted butter. Pack the butter into a small dish, cover it, and store it in the refrigerator.

Hibiscus Butter: Steep 2 tablespoons of crushed hibiscus flowers in 2 tablespoons of hot water for 10 minutes. Strain out and discard the flowers, and work the liquid and a pinch of salt into 1 stick (½ cup) of softened unsalted butter. Pack the butter into a small dish, cover it, and store it in the refrigerator.

Red Chili Butter: In a small bowl, smash ¼ to ½ teaspoon of your favorite chili powder and a pinch of salt into 1 stick (½ cup) of softened unsalted butter. Pack the butter into a small dish, cover it, and store it in the refrigerator.

Black Walnut Bread

Black walnuts are wild walnuts, indigenous to North America. They're different from those you buy in stores (English or Persian walnuts). Black walnuts taste far stronger—more concentrated and walnutty—and are a tad bitter. They take time and effort to first hull and then shell. Their aromas are lovely and nutty, and they add tremendous flavor to cookies and breads. Because black walnuts have a very high oil content, they are extremely perishable. Store them in the refrigerator or freezer.

Makes 2 round loaves

1½ cups chopped black walnuts or walnuts

1 packet (2¼ teaspoons) active dry yeast

2 teaspoons salt

3 tablespoons maple syrup

4 tablespoons walnut oil or olive oil

2 cups whole wheat flour

3 cups bread flour, plus a little more for kneading

Coarse cornmeal for dusting the baking sheet

Preheat the oven to 350 degrees. Scatter the walnuts on a baking sheet, and toast until they're fragrant, about 5 minutes. Set them aside to cool. Turn off the oven.

In a large mixing bowl, stir together the yeast, salt, and 2 cups of water. Stir in the maple syrup and 2 teaspoons of the oil.

Put 1 cup of the toasted walnuts into a food processor with 2 tablespoons of the whole wheat flour, and process until the walnuts are finely ground. Place the remaining whole wheat flour into the bowl with the yeast, and stir in the processed walnuts.

Add the 3 cups of bread flour a half cup at a time, stirring to form a dough that pulls away from the sides of the bowl. Turn the dough out onto a floured work surface and knead, dusting with additional bread flour as you go, until you have a soft, sticky dough, about 5 to 8 minutes.

Clean out the bowl, and coat it with about 1 tablespoon of the oil. Place the dough into the bowl, turning to coat it in oil. Cover the bowl with a clean dishcloth, and set aside to rise until the dough has doubled in size, about 1½ hours.

Punch down the dough, and add the remaining toasted walnuts, lightly kneading them into the dough. Dust a baking sheet with cornmeal. Divide the dough in half, shape it into two balls, and place them on the baking sheet. Cover the dough with the dishcloth, and allow it to rise for an hour.

Preheat the oven to 450 degrees. Slash the tops of the loaves about a half-inch deep with a razor or a sharp knife. Place the baking sheet in the oven. Bake for 20 minutes, then reduce the temperature to 350 degrees and continue baking until the loaves are well browned and sound hollow when tapped, about another 20 minutes. Cool the bread for at least 10 to 15 minutes before slicing it.

The Earth's Sweetest Gifts

DESSERTS

Strawberry shortcake, hand-cranked ice cream, grape dumplings—such sweet childhood memories. Mom and Grandma Peltier made amazing pies. I'm obsessed with chocolate and vanilla, two flavors most folks associate with Europe but whose origins are squarely in the Americas. I use these gifts from our ancestors with gratitude and respect.

Strawberry Blue Corn Shortcakes with Honeyed Cream

Serves 4

2 pints fresh garden strawberries, capped and sliced, or frozen berries thawed and chopped

¼ cup sugar

4 Blue Corn Biscuits (page 160)

Honeyed cream (see note)

Toss the strawberries with the sugar, and let them macerate while the biscuits warm.

Warm the biscuits in a low, 250-degree oven until it's time to serve. Remove the biscuits from the oven, split them in half, and place the bottom layer of each biscuit on a plate. Pile the biscuit halves with the strawberries and plenty of honeyed cream, and then place the top of each biscuit on the cream. Serve immediately.

Note: To make honeyed cream, whip ½ cup of heavy cream with 2 to 3 tablespoons of honey until stiff.

MEXICAN CHOCOLATE

Mexican chocolate is minimally processed, retaining much of its rustic flavor and texture. The slightly grainy texture distinguishes it from European style chocolate that is eaten primarily as candy. Mexican chocolate for beverages and savory dishes, *chocolate de mesa*, is sold in tablets.

Spicy Chocolate Bread Pudding

We created this decadent dessert to honor the Aztec emperor Montezuma, who, it's said, relied on a beverage of cacao and vanilla, sweetened with honey, for vigor. Legend has it that chocolate, a gift from the gods, is imbued with aphrodisiac, medicinal, and mystical qualities. I can attest that this special recipe makes a terrific Valentine's Day dessert. While it may look like a lot of steps, this rich, dense, chocolatey warm pudding is worth the effort.

Serves 8 to 10

3 whole dried pasilla peppers (sometimes called chile negro)

6 ounces good-quality, very dark chocolate (at least 70 percent cocoa), chopped

3 tablespoons unsalted butter, cut into bits, plus more for greasing the pan

3 cups whole milk

5 eggs

1 cup firmly packed brown sugar

½ teaspoon Mexican cinnamon (*canela*)

1 teaspoon allspice

1 tablespoon pure vanilla or vanilla bean paste

¼ cup dried cranberries

¼ cup dried tart cherries

9 to 10 ounces baguette or Chocolate Brioche (page 180), cut into 1-inch cubes

½ cup cacao nibs

1 cup chopped pecans

Honeyed cream (see note on page 177) or vanilla ice cream

Cilantro–Vanilla Bean Dessert Oil (page 235), for garnish

Open the chiles, discard the seeds and stems, and toast slightly by laying them in a skillet over medium-high heat and pressing them with a spatula until they sizzle. Turn and repeat on the other side. Transfer the chiles to a bowl, cover them with warm water, and let them soak until soft, about 30 minutes. Drain, and discard any leftover seeds, stems, and veins. Turn the chiles into a food processor fitted with a steel blade and puree. You should have about 2 to 3 tablespoons of puree.

Melt the chocolate and 3 tablespoons of butter in a small saucepan over low heat, stirring frequently. Remove and set aside.

In a large mixing bowl, whisk together the milk, eggs, brown sugar, cinnamon, allspice, vanilla, and chile puree. Slowly stir in the melted chocolate. Stir in the cranberries, cherries, bread, cacao nibs, and nuts. Smooth some plastic wrap onto the pudding, and set a small plate on top of it to weigh down the contents; keep the bread fully submerged for about 30 minutes or up to 2 hours.

Preheat the oven to 350 degrees. Generously butter 8 to 10 individual custard cups or a 10-inch-round, 2-inch-deep cake pan. Transfer the pudding into the pan or cups. If using custard cups, bake for 35 to 40 minutes; if using a pan, plan on 45 minutes. The pudding is ready when a toothpick inserted in the center comes out clean. Allow to cool slightly. Serve warm with honeyed cream or vanilla ice cream and garnished with a drizzle of the Cilantro–Vanilla Bean Dessert Oil.

Chocolate Brioche

Use this bread to double the chocolate wallop in Spicy Chocolate Bread Pudding (page 179) or serve it with a bowl of berries and honeyed cream (see note on page 177) or A-Maizing Corn Ice Cream (page 182).

Makes one 8 × 4 inch loaf

1½ teaspoons active dry yeast

2 tablespoons warm (110 degrees) water

2 tablespoons sugar

3 whole eggs

1½ teaspoons salt

2 cups flour

½ cup unsweetened cocoa powder

1 cup (2 sticks) unsalted butter, softened

Butter and flour an 8 × 4 inch loaf pan. Shake out any excess flour.

In a large bowl, stir together the yeast, water, and 1 tablespoon of the sugar. Let stand for 3 minutes.

In a separate bowl, whisk together the eggs, salt, and remaining 1 tablespoon of sugar. Add the yeast mixture, and stir in the flour and cocoa powder. Stir in the butter, and mix until the dough pulls away from the sides of the bowl. Form the dough into a log, and lift it into the loaf pan. Cover the pan, and allow the dough to rise until it's almost doubled in size, about 1 to 2 hours.

Preheat the oven to 375 degrees. Bake the loaf until it's golden brown and sounds hollow when tapped, about 35 to 45 minutes. Remove the bread from the oven, and allow it to cool about 5 minutes in the pan. Turn the loaf out onto a wire rack to cool.

Sweet Corn Granita

This simple corn granita calls for just three indigenous ingredients. Serve it with Very Berry Granita (page 185) and a few Crunchy Cornmeal Piñon Cookies (page 193).

Serves 4

6 ears sweet corn, shucked

½ cup agave syrup or maple syrup

Generous pinch salt

Mint sprigs, for garnish

Holding each ear upright, drag a fork through the kernels to break them up. Place the corn in a large pot, and add enough water just to cover the corn. (If necessary, cut the ears in half crosswise so they'll fit in the pot.) Bring the water to a boil, then reduce the heat to a simmer and cook the corn for 5 minutes. Let the corn cool in the water.

Hold the corn tip up and, using a sharp knife, slice the kernels from the cobs. Save the cobs for corn stock, and reserve the cooking water.

Place the kernels into a blender or a food processor fitted with a steel blade. Add 2 cups of the cooled corn water. Puree until the kernels are finely chopped. Transfer the puree to a large bowl. Add enough cooking water to the puree to make 3 cups, then stir in the agave syrup and season with salt. Chill the mixture in a refrigerator, then turn it into an ice cream maker and churn according to manufacturer's directions.

Alternately, pour the corn mixture into a 9 × 13 inch baking dish and freeze it until the edges become icy and the center is slushy, about 1 hour.

Using a fork, stir the edges into the middle of the pan. Repeat this step every 30 minutes until the granita is completely frozen, about 3 hours. When ready to serve, use the fork to scrape the granita into flaky ice crystals, then spoon it into bowls. Garnish with mint.

A-Maizing Corn Ice Cream

This sweet, creamy combo is reminiscent of the best sweet cornbread. Serve it garnished with fresh berries or on top of Spicy Chocolate Bread Pudding (page 179).

Serves 4 to 6

2 cups heavy cream

1 cup whole milk

½ cup maple syrup

1 teaspoon salt

5 ears sweet corn

6 large egg yolks

½ cup buttermilk

1 teaspoon pure vanilla

½ cup toasted corn kernels (see note), for garnish

In a medium saucepan, stir together the cream, milk, maple syrup, and salt, and set the pan over medium-low heat. Cut the kernels from the cobs, then break each cob in half. Add the kernels and the cobs to the cream. Bring the liquid to a boil, then remove the pan from the heat and allow the corn to steep for one hour.

Remove and discard the cobs. Pour the mixture into a blender, and puree on high. Pour the corn mixture back into the saucepan, and set it over medium-low heat. Put the egg yolks into a medium bowl and slowly whisk in ½ cup of the hot corn mixture. Pour the tempered egg mixture into the saucepan. Reduce the heat to low and cook, stirring constantly, until the mixture is thick enough to coat the back of a spoon.

Set a sieve over a medium bowl, and pour the mixture through the sieve to strain out the corn. Discard the corn, and stir the buttermilk and vanilla into the liquid. Put the bowl in the refrigerator to thoroughly chill. Pour the mixture into an ice cream maker and churn, following manufacturer's directions. Serve the ice cream garnished with toasted corn kernels.

Note: To toast corn kernels, preheat the oven to 400 degrees. Line a baking sheet with parchment paper. Scatter 1 cup of corn kernels on the baking sheet. (If using frozen corn, thaw and drain the kernels and pat them dry before roasting.) Roast the corn in the oven, turning several times, until the kernels are caramelized and very tender. Remove and cool.

Pine Needle Ice Cream

Pine needle syrup gives plain old vanilla ice cream a resinous kick. This syrup enhances cocktails and teas too. Serve this pretty green ice cream in a waffle cone, and you have a pine cone!

Serves 6 to 8

½ cup water

3 tablespoons agave syrup, honey, or maple syrup, or more to taste

Salt

½ cup spruce or Douglas fir needles

6 cups vanilla ice cream, softened

6 to 8 waffle cones

Put the water, agave syrup, and a pinch of salt into a saucepan, and bring the mixture to a boil for about 1 minute. Remove the pan from the heat, and add the pine needles. Steep the pine needles for at least 3 hours, or overnight. Pour the syrup into a colander set over a bowl, and strain out and discard the pine needles.

Scoop the softened ice cream into a bowl and, using a wooden spoon or a potato masher, work about ¼ cup of the syrup into the ice cream, adding more to taste. Store any remaining syrup in a covered container in the refrigerator. Serve the ice cream in waffle cones.

Classic Tapioca Brûlée

Tapioca, the base of this delicious pudding, is a gluten-free starch extracted from the cassava root. Indigenous to Brazil, cassava (aka yuca or manioc) thrives across South America. In this recipe, tapioca pearls create a creamy texture in a sweet pudding that comes together in a few minutes. Find tapioca pearls in the baking section of grocery stores and natural food co-ops. Serve topped with fresh berries and a drizzle of Prickly Pear Sauce (page 234).

Serves 4 to 6

½ cup (4 ounces) small pearl tapioca

2⅔ cups coconut milk or whole milk

⅓ cup honey or agave syrup

¼ teaspoon salt

½ teaspoon vanilla

Additional honey or a sprinkle of sugar, for the glaze

Fresh berries, for garnish

Put the tapioca and milk into a medium saucepan, and let the tapioca soak for 30 minutes. Stir in the honey and salt, set the pan over medium heat, and bring to a simmer. Reduce the heat to low, and simmer gently until the pearls become transparent and the mixture begins to thicken and the pearls begin to appear translucent, about 8 to 12 minutes, stirring frequently to keep the tapioca from sticking to the bottom. Remove the pan from the heat, and stir in the vanilla. Pour the pudding into individual cups or a bowl, allow to cool, then refrigerate until completely chilled, about 3 hours.

To glaze the pudding, preheat the broiler to high. Drizzle the honey (or a little sugar) over the top of the pudding, and smooth it into a thin layer. Run the custard under the broiler or use a small torch to caramelize the honey and create a dark crust.

Serve garnished with fresh berries.

Very Berry Granita

Make this refreshing dessert in the height of berry season using what you've picked fresh in your backyard, foraged along a wooded path, or found at the farmers market. A little orange juice goes a long way in amping up the flavors.

Serves 4 to 6

½ cup orange juice

3 to 4 tablespoons agave syrup or honey

1 pound mixed fresh or frozen berries (strawberries, raspberries, blackberries, etc.)

Mint sprigs, for garnish

In a blender or a food processor fitted with a steel blade, puree the orange juice, agave syrup, and berries until almost smooth. If the mixture seems to thick or clumpy, add a little water to thin it out. Taste, and adjust the sweetness.

Pour the berry mixture into a 9 × 13 inch baking dish, and freeze it until the edges become icy and the center is slushy, about 1 hour.

Using a fork, stir the edges into the middle of the pan. Repeat this step every 30 minutes until the granita is completely frozen, about 3 hours. When ready to serve, use the fork to scrape the granita into flaky ice crystals, then spoon it into bowls. Garnish with mint.

Grape Dumplings

In Oklahoma, every good cook has her own version of grape dumplings, a favorite treat. They were originally made with wild grapes, often called possum grapes because a cook needed to pick them before the possums did. Over time, the recipe has been adapted to use bottled Concord grape juice. As the dumplings cook, the grape juice simmers into a thick sauce. These are great topped with A-Maizing Ice Cream (page 235) or vanilla ice cream.

Serves 4 to 6

DUMPLINGS

- 1 cup all-purpose flour, plus a little more for dusting
- 1 tablespoon sugar
- 1½ teaspoons baking powder
- Pinch salt
- 2 tablespoons unsalted butter
- ½ cup Concord grape juice

POACHING LIQUID

- 3½ cups Concord grape juice

Dumplings: In a large bowl, whisk together the flour, sugar, baking powder, and salt. Cut in the butter with a pastry blender or your fingers until the mixture resembles small peas. Stir in the grape juice to make a stiff dough.

The dumplings can be formed in a variety of shapes, or simply rolled off a spoon into the poaching liquid. To roll and cut the dumplings, press the dough into a flat disk. Roll it out to about an inch thick, then use a very sharp knife to cut the dough into the desired shapes.

Poaching Liquid: Put the grape juice into a medium pot, set the pot over medium-low heat, and bring it to a simmer.

Drop the cut dumplings into the simmering liquid. If making drop dumplings, scoop and then drop teaspoons of the dumpling dough into the simmering liquid. Be careful not to crowd the pot. Stir once or twice, until the dumplings float to the surface, about 10 to 12 minutes. The grape juice will thicken into a sauce. Serve the dumplings warm, topped with the thickened poaching sauce and ice cream.

Sweet Corn and Butternut Squash Pudding

When it comes to old-fashioned corn pudding, this one is as easy and straightforward as it can get. It's made like polenta, but its origins date back to pre-European contact, and has been favored in tribal communities across the country. Like polenta, the cooked and cooled pudding can be cut into squares and fried. In this version, the pudding is a soft porridge with a creamy texture and the nutty sweet flavor of dried Iroquois heirloom corn. A splash of maple syrup and the roasted butternut squash elevate corn pudding to perfection. Serve it with a swirl of Cilantro–Vanilla Bean Dessert Oil (page 235) along with bright pops of fresh berries.

Serves 4 to 6

BUTTERNUT SQUASH

- 1 small butternut squash, sliced lengthwise and seeded
- Extra-virgin olive oil
- 2 tablespoons maple syrup

SWEET CORN PUDDING

- 1 cup coarse Iroquois toasted white or yellow cornmeal
- 2 cups water, more as needed
- 1 teaspoon fine salt
- 2 to 3 tablespoons agave syrup, honey, or maple syrup
- ½ cup corn kernels
- ¼ cup Cilantro–Vanilla Bean Dessert Oil (page 235)
- ½ cup fresh blueberries or raspberries, for garnish

Squash: Preheat the oven to 375 degrees. Line a baking sheet with parchment paper. Brush the squash with the oil and lay it cut-side down on the parchment. Roast the squash in the oven until it's very soft, about 25 to 30 minutes. When the squash is cool enough to handle, carefully scoop out the flesh into a bowl and discard the skin. Transfer the squash to a food processor fitted with a steel blade, add the maple syrup, and puree.

Corn Pudding: While the squash is roasting, make the corn pudding. Put the cornmeal, water, and salt into a heavy-bottomed saucepan and set it over medium heat. Bring to a simmer, and whisk constantly until the mush begins to thicken, about 5 minutes. Whisk in the agave syrup, and continue to whisk until the mush is thick, about 5 minutes more. Stir in the corn kernels. Remove the pan from the heat, and cover it to keep the pudding warm.

To assemble the dessert, spread the corn pudding out on a deep-sided platter and swirl the squash puree through the cornmeal pudding. Drizzle the Cilantro–Vanilla Bean Dessert Oil over all, and garnish with fresh berries.

Indian Pudding variation: This version of the corn pudding (aka cornmeal mush) is a North American classic. Europeans added milk or cream to the mush and then baked it off with a layer of cream on top to create a caramel crust. Serve this pudding warm.

Preheat the oven to 350 degrees. Prepare only the corn pudding portion of the recipe. Scoop the corn pudding into a baking dish, and pour ½ cup of heavy cream over the top so it puddles up in the shallows. Bake until the cream caramelizes, about 20 to 30 minutes. Serve warm with fresh berries.

Chocolate Obsession

Dense, chocolatey, and gluten free, this cake showcases the Indigenous gift of chocolate to the world. Use great-quality cocoa and chocolate. This cake is so rich that you'll want to serve each person a mere sliver.

Makes one 8-inch cake

1 cup bittersweet chocolate chips

½ cup (1 stick) unsalted butter, at room temperature

¾ cup granulated sugar

¼ teaspoon salt

2 teaspoons espresso powder

1 teaspoon vanilla extract

3 large eggs

½ cup Dutch process cocoa

Preheat the oven to 375 degrees. Lightly grease an 8-inch round cake pan, and line the bottom with a piece of parchment paper cut to fit.

Melt the chocolate and butter together in a small saucepan set over low heat, stirring constantly. Pour the chocolate mixture into a bowl. Stir in the sugar, salt, espresso powder, and vanilla. Whisk in the eggs and cocoa powder.

Spoon the batter into the pan, and bake the cake until the top forms a thin crust, about 25 minutes. Remove from the oven, and let the cake cool in the pan for 5 minutes. Loosen the edges of the pan with a butter knife and turn the cake out onto a plate. Allow the cake to cool.

PIÑON NUTS

The New Mexican piñon nut, harvested from indigenous trees, is smaller with a slightly different flavor than those imported from Italy. Piñon trees are small pine trees that grow in Arizona, New Mexico, Colorado, Nevada, and Utah. Most of the pine nuts in our stores are imported from Italy.

Crunchy Cornmeal Piñon Cookies

These golden pine nut sugar cookies are perfect with a strong cup of afternoon coffee or tea and make the perfect crumb crust for Pumpkin Cheesecake with Piñon Crust (page 194).

Makes about 3 dozen 2-inch cookies

½ cup (1 stick) unsalted butter

½ cup sugar

1 teaspoon vanilla extract

1 egg

2 egg yolks

1½ cups all-purpose flour

½ cup fine cornmeal

1 teaspoon baking powder

½ teaspoon salt

½ cup pine nuts

Preheat the oven to 325 degrees. Line a baking sheet with parchment paper.

In a large bowl, cream together the butter and sugar, then beat in the vanilla, egg, and egg yolks until incorporated.

In a medium bowl, stir together the flour, cornmeal, baking powder, and salt. Add the flour mixture to the butter mixture, stir combine, and then fold in the pine nuts. Using a tablespoon, drop the dough onto the baking sheet.

Bake until lightly browned, about 15 to 20 minutes. Remove and allow to cool slightly on the baking sheet before removing the cookies to a wire rack. Cool thoroughly before storing in an airtight container.

Pumpkin Cheesecake with Piñon Crust

Created for Corn Dance Café, this cheesecake is our Thanksgiving dessert.

Makes a 10-inch cheesecake

CRUST

1¼ cups crumbled Crunchy Cornmeal Piñon Cookies or firm sugar cookies

2 tablespoons unsalted butter, melted

FILLING

3 (8-ounce) packages cream cheese, at room temperature

1¾ cups sugar

1 teaspoon cinnamon

½ teaspoon allspice

½ teaspoon ground ginger

¼ cup all-purpose flour

1 teaspoon vanilla

1 cup pumpkin puree, canned pumpkin, or roasted pumpkin

5 large eggs

½ cup sour cream

Preheat the oven to 350 degrees. Lightly grease a 10-inch round springform pan with a little of the butter.

Crust: In the bowl of a food processor fitted with a steel blade, pulse together the cookies and butter. Press the cookie crumbs into the bottom of the springform pan and an inch up of the sides of the pan. Bake until the crust smells toasty, about 10 to 15 minutes. Remove the crust from the oven, and reduce the oven temperature to 300 degrees.

Filling: In a mixing bowl, beat the cream cheese until it's very creamy. Beat in the sugar, cinnamon, allspice, ginger, and flour until the mixture is very smooth, about 2 to 3 minutes. Beat in the vanilla and the pumpkin, then beat in the eggs one at a time. Stir in the sour cream. Pour the mixture into the prepared crust. Bake until the outer part of the cake is firm and the center is still a bit wobbly, about 50 to 60 minutes. Turn off the heat, prop open the oven door, and allow the cake to cool in the oven for about one hour. Remove the cake from the oven and chill, lightly covered, for at least 4 hours or longer before serving.

Apple Little Big Pies with Pecans

Try this sweet Little Big Pie with sliced pears or a mix of apple and pear slices. The sauce may be made ahead and held in the refrigerator for two days. Warm the sauce before serving it.

Makes six 9-inch pies

1 recipe Little Big Pie
  Dough (page 168)

12 tart apples, peeled, cored,
  and sliced ¼ inch thick

½ cup maple sugar or
  light brown sugar

½ cup heavy cream

¼ teaspoon vanilla extract

¼ cup chopped pecans

Preheat the oven to 400 degrees. Line two baking sheets with parchment paper.

Divide the Little Big Pie dough into six portions, and roll them out to 7-inch circles, each about an inch thick. Place the dough rounds on the baking sheets. Distribute the apple slices among the pies.

In a small dish, whisk together the maple sugar, heavy cream, and vanilla. Brush this mixture over the apples, and scatter the chopped pecans over the top of each pie. Bake until the crust is puffy and golden and the apples are tender, about 20 to 25 minutes.

Cranberry-Apricot Little Big Pies with Honey–Goat Cheese Cream

The bright cranberry-apricot topping is a nice contrast to the golden crust. Serve the pies topped with a dollop of the Honey–Goat Cheese Cream, and garnish them with chopped mint leaves.

Makes six 9-inch pies

1 recipe Little Big Pie Dough (page 168)

2 tablespoons unsalted butter

¼ cup honey, or more as needed

1 cup dried apricots

½ cup orange juice

1 cup cranberries

Honey–Goat Cheese Cream (page 235)

Chopped mint, for garnish

Preheat the oven to 400 degrees. Line two baking sheets with parchment paper.

Divide the Little Big Pie dough into six portions, and roll them out to 7-inch circles, each about an inch thick. Place the dough rounds on the baking sheets.

In a small saucepan or a microwave-safe bowl, melt the butter with 1 tablespoon of the honey. Brush the honey butter over the dough.

Put the apricots and orange juice into a small saucepan, set it over low heat, and simmer until the apricots have opened up and are very soft, about 10 to 15 minutes. Add a little water if the juice evaporates before the apricots are softened.

Put the cranberries into a separate saucepan, and add enough water to barely cover them. Set the pan over low heat, and cook until the cranberries have popped. Sweeten the cranberries to taste with the remaining honey, and continue simmering until the mixture is the consistency of jam.

Spoon the apricot mixture across the pies, then spoon the cranberries over the apricots. Bake until the dough is golden and the pie tops are bubbly. Remove and let cool about 10 minutes before serving. Serve garnished with Honey–Goat Cheese Cream and chopped mint.

Pecan Dessert Sauce

This is my go-to dessert sauce. So delicious and rich, it's practically a candy itself. You can spoon it over ice cream and tapioca pudding, or reduce the liquid so that it's firm enough to spoon into candy cups. This sauce will keep in the refrigerator for up to 3 weeks in a covered container.

Makes 2½ cups

1 cup packed dark brown sugar

½ cup water

¼ teaspoon white vinegar

2 tablespoons chopped toasted pecans

½ cup cream

2 tablespoons cream cheese

½ teaspoon vanilla

In a small pot set over low heat, dissolve the sugar in the water and vinegar. Stir in the nuts. Increase the heat to medium, and cook until the mixture thickens, about 5 minutes. Slowly stir in the cream, cream cheese, and vanilla. Pour the syrup into a container. When cooled completely, cover and store the sauce in the refrigerator.

Pralines

Gift these to your friends at Christmas, but be warned, they may come to expect them *every* year.

Makes about twenty-four 2-inch pralines

2 cups light brown sugar

¾ cup heavy cream

4 tablespoons unsalted butter

⅛ teaspoon baking soda

2 cups pecan or walnut halves

½ teaspoon salt

1 teaspoon vanilla

Line two baking sheets with parchment paper.

Put the brown sugar, cream, butter, and baking soda into a pot. Set the pot over medium heat, and stir constantly until the mixture begins to foam and boil. Continue stirring until the mixture reaches 240 degrees. Remove the pan from the heat, and add the pecans, salt, and vanilla. Continue stirring until the mixture thickens, about 3 to 4 minutes. Working quickly, drop spoonfuls of the mixture onto parchment paper. When the pralines are cool and firm, store them in an airtight container.

Nature's Refreshments

TEAS AND SPIRITS

At Thirty Nine Restaurant, we offer teas made with locally sourced ingredients as well as a selection of cocktails, local beers, and wines, many of them from our Indigenous vintners. Tribes in California, New Mexico, Utah, and British Columbia have created small, successful, critically acclaimed wines. They incorporate strict sustainability practices in an effort to protect the land. (See Sources, page 237.)

Five Honest Teas

Our tribal elders had no need for pharmacies and prescriptions. They seemed to know exactly what our bodies required, especially when the seasons changed. Often, it was a tea sourced from the plants that grew outside our door or were discovered along our wooded trails. Here are recipes for the delicious and soothing teas we serve at Thirty Nine Restaurant.

CORN SILK TEA

Save the corn silk from your shucked corn, and roll it into bundles roughly the size of your thumb. Or wrap the silk around your thumb, lay out the little coils, and let them dry. Store the dried corn silk in a plastic bag or on string or kitchen twine.

Figuring one small bundle per serving, put the corn silk into a saucepan, and add 1 cup of water per serving. Bring the water to a boil, then turn off the heat and let the corn silk steep for about 5 minutes. Strain out and discard the corn silk. Sweeten the tea to taste.

HIBISCUS FLOWER (JAMAICA) TEA

This is our house tea at Thirty Nine Restaurant. It's a gorgeous bright magenta color, tangy, floral, refreshing and light. To make 1 cup of tea, put 2 to 3 tablespoons of dried hibiscus flowers and a cup of water in a pot. Set the pot over low heat, and simmer for about 15 minutes. Strain out and discard the flowers. Sweeten the tea with honey; it's fabulous cold or hot.

PINE TIP TEA

Plan on ¼ cup of pine needles per cup of tea. Put the pine needles and 1 cup of water per serving into a saucepan. Bring the water to a boil, turn off the heat and let the pine needles steep for about 5 minutes. Strain out and discard the pine needles. Sweet to taste.

Note: Do *not* make tea out of anything you cannot identify. Some evergreens, such as cypress and yew are toxic. Do *not* drink pine needle tea if you are pregnant or nursing.

ROSE HIP TEA

Plan on ½ cup of fresh rose hips or 1 heaping tablespoon of dried rose hips per cup of tea. Put the rose hips into a saucepan, and add 1 cup of water per serving. Bring the water to a boil, then turn off the heat and let the rose hips steep for about 5 minutes. Strain out and discard the rose hips. Sweeten to taste.

SUMAC TEA, OR INDIAN LEMONADE

Place 3 to 6 clusters of dried sumac berries into a plastic bag and crush them, or use a mortar and pestle, and then sift out and discard the big pieces. Place the crushed berries into a pitcher or a bowl, and add 8 to 12 cups of cold water. Soak the crushed sumac berries for 12 hours. Set a fine sieve over a bowl, and pour the liquid through the sieve. Discard the sumac berries. Sweeten the lemonade to taste, and serve it warm or cold.

Sangrita

This traditional Mexican drink is served as a chaser to high-end tequilas and was a signature drink at Corn Dance Café. It doesn't contain alcohol, so sangrita makes a fabulous virgin cocktail for sipping at the bar. It's meant to cleanse and brighten the palate between sips of tequila. Spicy, sweet, and savory, it's served in a little pony glass.

Makes 2½ cups

11 ounces tomato juice
   (not vegetable juice)

10 ounces orange juice

 2 ounces fresh lime juice

 4 dashes Tabasco

   Pinch salt

   Dash of agave syrup
   or maraschino syrup

Mix all the ingredients together well with a little ice, then strain the sangrita into salt-rimmed glasses or a small pitcher.

Prickarita (Prickly Pear Margarita)

Pretty as a desert sunset, this is a special drink that must be served in a wide-mouth, long-stemmed glass; it's a classic cocktail from the Corn Dance Café menu.

Makes 1 drink

3 ounces tequila blanco

½ ounce Cointreau

1½ ounces lime juice

2 ounces Prickly Pear Sauce (page 234)

Kosher salt and turbinado sugar for rimming the glass

Combine the tequila, Cointreau, lime juice, Prickly Pear Sauce, and a little crushed ice in a cocktail shaker and shake. Put a few tablespoons of salt and sugar into a dish. Wet the rim of a margarita glass, then dip it into the salt and sugar mixture. Strain the chilled prickarita into the glass, and serve right away.

~~~~~~

INDIAN LEMONADE

Staghorn Sumac, aka North American wild sumac, grows throughout Michigan, the Great Lakes, and Oklahoma. Its flavor is mildly lemony and tart; it's often used in spice mixes, simmered as tea, or made into a refreshing drink reminiscent of lemonade.

Sumac is easy to identify—the cone-shaped cluster of berries stands up straight from the branches like a stag's horn. Sumac is loaded with antioxidant properties and lots of vitamin C. It has been used by Natives for eons to treat colds, sore throats, fevers, and asthma. It's known to lower blood sugar and can aide in managing diabetes.

~~~~~~

～～～～～～～～～～～～～～～～

MEXICAN HOT CHOCOLATE

The Che'il Mayan Chocolate company, one of the first cacao plantations to also manufacture chocolate, was founded by Julio Saqui in Belize. The master chocolate maker offers farm-to-factory tours that reveal the intricate, careful work of using traditional, sustainable, organic practices to create distinctively delicious chocolate. Though this special chocolate is not yet available in the United States, please check out Sources (page 237) for the brands made with integrity that are sold here.

Ancient Mayan chocolate drinks were a blend of ground cocoa seeds, cornmeal, and chile pepper, simmered together and then mixed until foamy and served in golden goblets to the wealthy.

～～～～～～～～～～～～～～～～

Mexican Hot Cocoa

No matter how well your milk and chocolate are blended, some solids will settle in the bottom of the cup. Serve this drink with a cinnamon stick, or *canela*, for stirring. You can find Mexican cocoa disks, *chocolate de mesa*, at many ethnic grocery stores, natural food co-ops, and online (see Sources, page 237). Use an immersion blender for maximum frothing.

Serves 3 to 4

3 ounces Mexican
   table chocolate

4 cups whole milk

1 to 2 drops vanilla

   Dash of ground cinnamon

Divide the chocolate into wedges, then chop it. Pour the milk into a saucepan, and set it over medium heat. Once the first tiny bubbles begin to appear in the milk, whisk in the chocolate and continue stirring, slowly and constantly, until the chocolate has melted. Don't let the milk boil; stir in the vanilla. If desired, froth the hot chocolate with an immersion blender or a milk frother. Serve the hot cocoa in mugs, garnished with a sprinkle of cinnamon and a cinnamon stick for stirring.

Mexican Coffee

In Mexica, cinnamon (*canela*) and unrefined sugar (*piloncillo*) are brewed right into the coffee, not added later. The result is a sweet, spicy coffee that's delicious garnished with an orange peel. This is best made with a French press.

Makes about 6 to 8 cups

8 cups water

4 ounces piloncillo (see note) or ½ cup brown sugar

⅔ cup medium grind, dark roast coffee

1 cinnamon stick

Peel of 1 orange

Bring the water to a boil in a medium saucepan. Add the piloncillo, and stir to dissolve. Add the coffee, cinnamon stick, and orange peel. Turn off the heat, cover the pot, and steep for 10 minutes. Remove the cinnamon stick and orange peel. Pour the brew into a French press, and filter out the grounds. Serve the coffee garnished with cinnamon sticks.

Note: Piloncillo is unrefined sugar cane often sold in small cones in Mexican grocery stores. Brown sugar makes an acceptable substitute.

Preserving the Best

No guest leaves my home without a jar of homemade jam, jelly, or pickles. Having a few of these on hand is a bonus for any home cook; they can dress up the simplest meal. A drizzle of Rose Hip Sauce (page 229) brightens up sautéed turkey medallions and is delicious over roasted fish. Do try the Pineapple Serrano Salsa (page 233) on grilled meats or with a bowl of chips. I can't eat turkey or duck without a dollop of Gingery Cranberry Jam (page 217).

Loretta's Quick Pickles

Come August, my Mom and my Grandmothers spent hours in the sweltering kitchen putting up pickles, jellies, and jams. Here's a quick pickle recipe that brings the same snappy condiments to the table in far less time. Store these pickles in the refrigerator for up to 2 weeks. I make these pickles with thinly sliced zucchini to serve on burgers at Thirty Nine Restaurant.

Makes about 1 quart

2 cups rice vinegar

1½ cups sugar

2 tablespoons lime juice

2 tablespoons coarse salt

¼ cup water

1 jalapeño, seeded
  and thinly sliced

4 cucumbers, sliced
  ¼-inch thick

1 carrot, thinly sliced

3 cloves garlic, peeled

In a small saucepan, simmer the vinegar, sugar, lime juice, salt, and water until the sugar and salt have dissolved. Allow the liquid to cool to room temperature. Put the jalapeño, cucumbers, carrot, and garlic into a large bowl and then pour in the pickling liquid. Cover and chill for at least 4 hours.

Transfer the pickles into clean jars, and store them in the refrigerator for up to 3 weeks.

Mom's Famous Chile Sauce (Piccalilli)

Piccalilli, aka chow-chow, is a tomato relish. This is my Mom's amazing recipe, and we slather this Okie favorite on sausages, brisket, game, and burgers. The combination of green tomatoes, onions, and bell and hot peppers is tangy, sweet, and spicy. It makes great use of end-of-season green tomatoes that won't have time to ripen.

Makes 3 pints

15 to 20 medium green
   tomatoes, peeled
   and chopped

1 cup chopped green
   bell pepper

1 cup chopped onion

1 jalapeño or serrano pepper,
   seeded and chopped

1 tablespoon celery seed

2 teaspoons mustard seed

1 small bay leaf

½ teaspoon whole cloves

½ teaspoon ground ginger

½ teaspoon ground nutmeg

1 small cinnamon stick

½ cup brown sugar

1½ cups cider vinegar

1 tablespoon salt

Put the tomatoes, bell peppers, onion, and jalapeño in a large pot. Put the celery seed, mustard seed, bay leaf, cloves, ginger, nutmeg, and cinnamon stick into a spice bag and add it to the tomato mixture. Set the pot over high heat and bring the mixture to a boil, then reduce the heat and simmer until the mixture is reduce by half, stirring frequently, about 20 to 30 minutes. Stir in the sugar, vinegar, and salt. Increase the heat and bring to a boil for 5 minutes. Remove the spice bag. Transfer the piccalilli into clean jars and allow the piccalilli to cool.

Store the piccalilli in covered containers in the refrigerator for up to 3 weeks.

Gingery Cranberry Jam

I can't imagine eating turkey or duck without this on the side; it's a must at Thanksgiving. Our indigenous wild ginger, aka snakeroot, is now being cultivated on smaller local farms and comes into season in late summer. Look for it in our farmers markets.

Makes 2 half-pints

4 cups cranberries

2-inch piece fresh ginger, grated

1 tablespoon lime juice, or to taste

½ cup honey or maple syrup, or to taste

¼ cup water

Put all of the ingredients into a small saucepan, and set it over medium heat. Bring the liquid to a simmer, and cook until the cranberries pop. Remove from the heat, and let the jam cool to room temperature before transferring it to containers and covering.

Store the jam in the refrigerator for up to a month, or freeze it.

Loretta's Fierce Tomato Jam

When I'm blessed with a bumper crop of tomatoes, I make this spicy-sweet jam. You can use any tomatoes you have on hand, though I've found the oblong Roma tomatoes work best.

Makes about 2 half-pints

1½ pounds ripe tomatoes, seeded and chopped

1 cup sugar

2 tablespoons lime juice

1 tablespoon grated fresh ginger

1 teaspoon ground cumin

¼ teaspoon ground cinnamon

¼ teaspoon ground allspice

1 teaspoon salt

1 small jalapeño or serrano pepper, seeded and minced

Put all of the ingredients into a heavy medium saucepan, and set it over medium heat. Bring to a simmer, and cook, stirring occasionally, until the mixture reaches a thick, jammy consistency, about 45 minutes to 1 hour. Taste, and adjust the seasoning. Cool the jam before transferring it to containers and covering. Store the jam in the refrigerator for up to 2 weeks.

Any Fruit Jam

Our sons would pick every berry vine clean, climb into the crabapple trees, or clamber over to grab the biggest peaches off the tree. Here is the basic jam recipe I used to dispatch those very fresh fruits.

I prefer *not* to give this jam a water bath once it's cooked. Why cook already-cooked fruit a second time? Instead, I store the jam in the refrigerator or freezer; it is not shelf stable.

Makes about 4 to 6 half-pints

4 pounds whole blueberries, blackberries, strawberries, or peaches

3 cups sugar

3 to 4 tablespoons fresh lemon or lime juice

Prepare the fruit by stemming, peeling, and pitting as needed and, if the fruit is large, cutting it into 1-inch pieces. Put the fruit, sugar, and lemon juice into a heavy saucepan, and allow the fruit to macerate overnight at room temperature.

Set the pot over medium heat, and bring it to a simmer. Cook, stirring very gently, until the juices begin to boil, about 15 minutes. Increase the heat to medium-high and cook, stirring frequently to prevent the jam from sticking and burning on the bottom of the pot. The juices will thicken as the liquid evaporates and the fruit breaks down, about 40 to 50 minutes (timing will depend on the fruit's ripeness).

When the jam is thick, remove the pot from the heat and divide the jam among clean canning jars, leaving ¼ inch of head space in each jar. Allow the jam to cool to room temperature and then cover it. Store the jam in the refrigerator, or freeze it.

Sand Plum Jelly

Sand plums, aka Chickasaw plums, are round, tiny, cherry-like, and very tart. They grow across much of the central and western states, preferring dry, sandy soil, prairies, and pastures. Their pretty white blooms appear early in the season. As a kid, I'd go with my Grandmothers and Aunts out to tag the thickets, tying ribbons around their branches so in the fall, we'd find where the good picking might be. Picking sand plums was a communal affair among the women in the tribe. But once the plums were harvested and divvied up, the competition to make the clearest jelly was fierce. Grandma's jelly was good, but never, in her estimation, quite clear enough. Mom's jelly was the best! Here's the recipe, but, to be honest, I often buy it online (see Sources, page 237).

Makes about 8 pints

5 pounds wild plums, halved and pitted

4 cups water

1 (1¾-ounce) package powdered pectin

7 cups sugar

Put the plums and water into a stockpot, set it over high heat, and bring the water to a boil. Then reduce the heat, and simmer until the plums tender, about 30 minutes. Line a sieve with cheesecloth, and set it over a large bowl. Pour the plum mixture into the strainer, and let it stand until the liquid measures about 5½ cups, about 30 minutes (see note).

Return the liquid to the pan. Add the pectin, stir, and bring the liquid to a boil. Stir in the sugar and, stirring constantly, let the liquid boil for 1 minute.

Remove the pot from the heat, and skim off the foam. Carefully ladle the mixture into clean jars, leaving ¼ inch of headspace in each jar. Allow the jelly to cool before tightening the lids. Store the jelly in the refrigerator for up to a month, or freeze it.

Note: The trick to making clear jelly is to never mash or press the plum mixture through the cheesecloth. You need to be patient and let it drip, drip, drip.

Hot Honey

Drizzle this honey over corn sticks and cornbread, slather it on biscuits. Adjust the heat to your liking.

Makes 1 half-pint

8 ounces clover or other mild honey

1 jalapeño or serrano pepper, seeded, deveined, and sliced in half, or 1 tablespoon red pepper flakes

Put the honey and the pepper into a small saucepan. Set the pan over low heat, and bring the honey to a simmer. Turn off the heat, and allow the pepper to flavor the honey for 20 minutes about 20 minutes. Strain out the pepper, and decant the honey into a jar.

Lime variation: Stir in a tablespoon or two of lime juice, and add a thin slice of lime to the jar.

Chimichurri Sauce

This fiery, tangy, herbaceous sauce is meant for rich meats. It makes a wonderful marinade for wild game and red meat headed to the grill, then use it to baste the meat as it cooks.

Makes about 2 cups

1 jalapeño, seeded and finely chopped

5 cloves garlic, chopped

½ cup red wine vinegar

1 teaspoon salt

½ cup finely chopped cilantro

¼ cup finely chopped parsley

2 tablespoons finely chopped oregano, Mexican if available

¾ cup extra-virgin olive oil

Salt

In a medium bowl, whisk together the jalapeño, garlic, vinegar, and salt. Let the mixture sit for about 10 minutes. Stir in the cilantro, parsley, and oregano, then whisk in the oil in a slow, steady stream. Season the sauce to taste with salt.

Store the sauce in a covered container in the refrigerator for up to 5 days.

Chipotle Mayonnaise

This will be your new go-to spread for sandwiches and the base for delicious dips and dressings.

Makes about 1¼ cups

1 cup good-quality
   mayonnaise (such
   as Hellman's)

2 cloves garlic, minced

2 to 3 teaspoons
   fresh lime juice

½ teaspoon chipotle spice,
   or more to taste

Salt

Put the ingredients into a small bowl, and whisk to combine them. Store the mayonnaise in a covered container in the refrigerator for up to 2 weeks.

Chipotle Oil

Whisk this oil into vinaigrettes, and drizzle it over corn and roasted potatoes and sweet potatoes. While many recipes call for canned chipotles in adobo, they seldom call for the sauce. This recipe makes great use of that leftover adobo sauce.

Makes 1 cup

1 cup extra-virgin olive oil

1 to 2 tablespoons adobo
   sauce from canned
   chipotles in adobo

In a small bowl, whisk the ingredients together. Store in a covered container in the refrigerator for up to 2 months.

Two Pestos

These two pestos make a fabulous garnish on grilled bison, duck, and fish. Toss them with pasta or over roasted vegetables. Store them in covered containers the refrigerator for up to a week, or freeze them.

Makes about ¾ cup

SAGE PESTO

1 clove garlic

1 cup fresh sage leaves

¼ cup flat-leaf parsley leaves

Coarse salt

½ cup piñon nuts, lightly toasted (see note)

¼ cup extra-virgin olive oil

Juice of 1 lemon

In a food processor fitted with a steel blade, pulse together the garlic, sage, parsley, salt, and piñon nuts until they form a paste. Gradually process in the oil, then taste and adjust the seasonings.

Note: To toast the nuts, put then into a small pan and set it over low heat. Toast, shaking the pan occasionally, until they turn golden brown, about 3 to 5 minutes.

Makes about 1 cup

PUMPKIN SEED PESTO

1 clove garlic

1 cup flat-leaf parsley leaves

3 sage leaves

Generous pinch coarse salt

3 tablespoons unsalted, plain pumpkin seeds

⅓ cup extra-virgin olive oil

In a food processor fitted with a steel blade, pulse together the garlic, parsley, sage, salt, and pumpkin seeds until a paste forms. Gradually process in the oil, then taste and adjust the seasonings.

Creamed Garlic

This stores beautifully in the refrigerator and is terrific as that "shot of something" when a dish needs a boost. For more a robust, slightly sweeter Creamed Garlic, consider roasting the garlic as the first step. Serve this sauce on grilled chicken, fish, and game.

Makes 1½ cups

½ cup peeled garlic cloves

1 teaspoon coarse salt

1 cup extra-virgin olive oil

Shot of lemon juice

Turn the garlic cloves and salt into a food processor fitted with a steel blade. Process until the garlic is finely minced, about 1 minute, scraping down the sides as necessary.

With the food processor running, pour in one to two tablespoons of the oil. Scrape down the bowl, and then continue adding the oil a tablespoon or two at a time until the mixture looks creamy.

Once the garlic looks emulsified, begin adding more oil along with lemon juice to taste, until the oil has been processed in. Transfer to a glass container and store, covered, in the refrigerator for up to 3 months.

Tangy Sauce for Fish

This sauce keeps nicely in the refrigerator. It's great over grilled chicken too.

Makes about 1 cup

2 cups Best Vegetable Stock (page 68)

2 tablespoons rice wine vinegar

2 tablespoons brown sugar

¼ cup chopped mint

Salt to taste

In a medium pot, bring the vegetable stock to a boil, then reduce the heat and simmer until reduced by half. You should have about 1 cup of liquid or less. Whisk in the vinegar, sugar, and mint.

This sauce keeps beautifully when refrigerated in a covered container for up to 3 weeks.

Roasted Red Pepper Sauce

This is a wonderfully rich, deeply flavored sauce. The peppers are first grilled or broiled, then cooked with olive oil, garlic, and chile flakes. The sauce is just right drizzled over rabbit and wonderful on chicken and grilled fish. The recipe is easily doubled.

Makes about 1 cup

2 large red bell peppers (about 1 pound)

1 tablespoon extra-virgin olive oil

2 large cloves garlic, smashed

Salt

Generous pinch red pepper flakes

To roast the peppers, place them directly on the flame of a gas stovetop or under a broiler. Using tongs, roll them constantly until the skins are blackened. Put the peppers into a small brown paper bag or wrap them in a clean towel to cool. Then, holding a pepper over a bowl to capture its juice, rub the blackened skins from the pepper. Remove the veins and seeds from the peppers and dice them.

Film a skillet with the oil, add the garlic, a pinch of salt, the peppers and any juices you collected, and some red pepper flakes. Bring the sauce to a simmer, and stir until the peppers are extremely tender and the liquid has cooked off. Transfer this mixture to a food processor or a blender, and puree it into a sauce.

Refrigerate the sauce in a covered container for up to a month in the refrigerator.

Sour Cherry Sauce

This sauce is lovely spooned over grilled wild game, chicken, and roasted duck.

Makes about 1½ cups

3 cups pitted sour cherries

¼ cup honey or maple syrup

2 teaspoons balsamic vinegar

Place the cherries and honey in a small saucepan, and set it over medium heat. Using the back of a fork, mash the cherries slightly to release their juices. Simmer, stirring occasionally, until the cherries begin to soften. Stir in the vinegar.

The sauce will keep about 1 month in a covered jar in the refrigerator.

ROSE HIPS

Rose hips are the fruit, or seed pods, of rose plants. Typically orange, sometimes purple or black, they ripen in the late summer or fall, after the rose blossoms have faded and their petals dropped.

If you leave the spent flowers on the rose bush, you'll see the small, berry-sized hips left on the tips of the stems. The birds love them, and I do too. The rose is in the same family as the crab apple. Rose hips are tart and a great source of vitamin C. They're wonderful brewed into a pretty red, tangy tea or simmered into sauces and syrups.

Rose Hip Sauce

This is my go-to sauce for fish, and it's great on game too. Try it whisked into a vinaigrette then drizzled over wild rice for a lively grain salad.

Makes about ½ cup

1 cup Best Vegetable
   Stock (page 68)

1 teaspoon balsamic vinegar

2 teaspoons maple syrup
   or brown sugar

1 tablespoon fresh
   orange juice

2 teaspoons orange zest

¼ cup dried rose hips

   Pinch salt

In a small saucepan, bring the stock, vinegar, maple syrup, orange juice and zest, rose hips, and salt to a boil. Reduce the heat, and simmer until it's cooked down into a light syrup, about 5 to 10 minutes. Remove from the heat, then strain out and discard the rose hips.

Store, covered, in the refrigerator for up to 3 weeks.

Sweet and Sassy Rose Hip Sauce

This tangy, sweet sauce perks up savory and sweet dishes. It's as delicious drizzled over grilled meat and fish as it is over ice cream or Pumpkin Cheesecake with Piñon Crust (page 194). Try a few tablespoons in a cocktail or hot tea.

Makes 1 cup

1 cup dried whole or cut
   and sifted rose hips

1 tablespoon orange zest

2 cups water

1 tablespoon honey,
   or more to taste

In a nonreactive saucepan, simmer the rose hips and orange zest in the 2 cups of water for about 5 minutes. Remove the pan from the heat, and let stand for 5 minutes. Turn the pan's contents into a sieve set over a bowl. Strain out and discard the pulp, pressing with the back of a spoon to release all the liquid. Return the liquid to the saucepan, add the honey, and simmer until the liquid has reduced by half. Turn the sauce into a jar, and add more honey to taste.

Store, covered, in the refrigerator for up to 3 months.

Loretta's Magic Salt

This is my go-to seasoning when whatever I'm making just needs a pinch of something!

Makes 1 cup

- 1 cup Maldon or Alaska Pure Sea Salt (see Sources, page 237)
- 1 tablespoon chopped parsley
- 1 tablespoon chopped sage
- 1 teaspoon red pepper flakes
- 1 teaspoon juniper berries
- 1 teaspoon red pepper berries

Put the ingredients into a food processor fitted with a steel blade and pulse together. Store the seasoned salt in a jar with a lid.

Pineapple Serrano Salsa

This salsa will keep several days in the refrigerator. Serve it with chips, on burgers, and over grilled meats.

Makes about 3 cups

2 cups chopped fresh
  pineapple

1 small red onion, minced

½ cup minced red bell pepper

¼ cup minced green
  bell pepper

1 clove garlic, minced

2 tablespoons chopped basil

½ cup chopped cilantro

¼ cup chopped mint

1 serrano chile, seeded
  and chopped

1 teaspoon red pepper flakes

½ teaspoon toasted cumin
  (see note on page 62)

¼ cup lime juice

Salt to taste

Put all of the ingredients into a nonreactive bowl, and toss them together. Store the salsa in a covered container in the refrigerator.

Prickly Pear Sauce

This beautiful purple-red sauce is fabulous over A-Maizing Corn Ice Cream (page 182) or drizzled on Pumpkin Cheesecake with Piñon Crust (page 194), Classic Tapioca Brûlée (page 186), and Chocolate Obsession (page 190).

This sauce will keep in the refrigerator for several weeks in a covered container, and it freezes nicely. As a backup, stock up on prickly pear puree from Perfect Puree in Napa (see Sources, page 237).

Makes about 2 cups

2½ pounds prickly pears
⅓ cup agave syrup or sugar
1 tablespoon fresh
  lime juice

Cut ½ inch off both ends of the prickly pears, then make a ½-inch deep incision down the side of each one. Carefully peel off the rind, starting from the incision: the rind is thick and, if the fruit is ripe, will peel easily away from the central core. Roughly chop the peeled prickly pears, then put them into a food processor fitted with a steel blade and puree. Pour into a strainer set over a bowl. You should have 3 cups of juice in the bowl.

In a medium-sized saucepan, combine 2 cups of the juice with the agave syrup and set the pan over medium heat. Simmer, stirring frequently, until the liquid is reduced to 1 cup, about 5 to 10 minutes. Cool to room temperature.

Pour the cooked mixture into a bowl with the remaining 1 cup of juice and season with the lime juice. Store in a covered container or squeeze bottle in the refrigerator.

Cilantro–Vanilla Bean Dessert Oil

This emerald-green oil is a total surprise. Honey sweetened, spiked with coriander and allspice, it awakens the flavors of corn and squash desserts. Try it on vanilla ice cream or over Classic Tapioca Brûlée (page 186). Store the oil in a covered container in the refrigerator for up to a week.

Makes about 1¼ cups

1 cup extra-virgin olive oil

1 bunch cilantro leaves, destemmed

½ teaspoon ground coriander

¼ teaspoon ground allspice

1 tablespoon honey

½ teaspoon vanilla extract

Seeds from 1 vanilla bean or 1 tablespoon vanilla bean paste

In a food processor fitted with a steel blade or a blender, pulse together the oil and the cilantro. Turn the oil into a fine mesh sieve set over a bowl. Strain out and discard the cilantro leaves. Add the coriander, allspice, honey, vanilla extract, and vanilla seeds, and mix well. Pour the oil into a squeeze bottle with a fine tip. Use droplets on dessert plates and over puddings, cakes, and ice cream.

Honey–Goat Cheese Cream

I created this sauce for sweet Little Big Pies (pages 195–96), and it's great drizzled over a bowl of fruit too.

Makes about ⅓ cup

½ cup chèvre

1 to 2 tablespoons honey

2 tablespoons sour cream

In a small bowl, whisk together the ingredients. Store the cream in a covered container in the refrigerator for up to 3 week

Sources of Selected Ingredients

ALMONDS
Seka Hills, sekahills.com

BALSAMIC VINEGAR
Seka Hills, sekahills.com

BEANS, HERITAGE DRIED
Rancho Gordo, ranchogordo.com

BEANS, TEPARY, BLACK, PINTO
Ramona Farms, ramonafarms.com

BISON PRODUCTS
Tankabar, tankabar.com

BISON
Northstar Bison, northstarbison.com

BLACK WALNUTS
Hammonds Black Walnuts, black-walnuts.com

CAVIAR
North American Caviar, northamericancaviar.com

CHILES
The Spice House, thespicehouse.com

CRANBERRIES, UNSWEETENED, DRIED
Honestly Cranberries, honestlycranberry.com

CRAWFISH (FRESH OR FROZEN)
Louisiana Crawfish Co, lacrawfish.com

FISH, FRESHWATER (WALLEYE, TROUT)
Red Lake Nation Fishery, redlakednr.org/fisheries

FLOUR
Shawnee Milling Company, shawneemilling.com

FRUIT PUREES
Perfect Puree of Napa Valley, perfectpuree.com

GAME
Indian Valley Meats, indianvalleymeats.com

HERBS AND SPICES
Rancho Gordo, ranchogordo.com

HERBS, ASSORTED
Spice Island Blends, spiceislands.com

HERBS, FINE
Spice Island Blends, spiceislands.com

HERITAGE CORN, CORN MEAL, POLENTA, GRITS
Ramona Farms, ramonafarms.com

HERITAGE WHEAT BERRIES AND FLOUR
Ramona Farms, ramonafarms.com

HICKORY NUTS
Foraged Market, foraged.market/shop
/specialty-produce/nuts-and-seeds
/wild-foraged-hickory-nuts-shelled

**IROQUOIS WHITE CORN FLOUR,
CORNMEAL, GRITS, GANONDAGAN**
ganondagan.org/whitecorn/about

LAMB, CHURRO
Heritage Belle Farms,
heritagebellefarms.com/lamb

**MAYAN CHOCOLATE, COFFEE,
CINNAMON, ETC.**
Che'il Mayan Chocolate Company
products distributor

MEXICAN CHOCOLATE
Taza, tazachocolate.com

MEXICAN CINNAMON (CANELA)
Slofoodgroup, slofoodgroup.com

NATIVE PINE NUTS (PIÑON)
Pinenut Company, pinenut.com

NOPALES (PRICKLY PEAR CACTUS)
Melissa's Produce, Melissas.com

OLIVE OIL
Seka Hills, sekahills.com

OREGANO
Slofoodgroup, slofoodgroup.com

PRICKLY PEAR PUREE
Perfect Puree of Napa Valley, perfectpuree.com

ROSE HIPS
Mountain Rose Herbs, mountainroseherbs.com

SAND PLUM JELLY
Southern Roots Sisters, southernrootssisters.com

SPICE BLENDS
Mountain Rose Herbs, mountainroseherbs
.com; The Spice House, thespicehouse.com

VANILLA BEAN PASTE
Slofoodgroup, slofoodgroup.com

VINEGARS, PINEAPPLE AND BANANA
Rancho Gordo, ranchogordo.com

WALNUTS
Seka Hills, sekahills.com

WILD RICE
Native Harvest, nativeharvest.com/products
/manoomin-wild-rice; Moose Lake Wild
Rice Company, mooslakewildrice.com

YELLOW AND WHITE CORNMEAL
Shawnee Milling Company, shawneemilling.com

Index

References to recipes appear in **bold** type. References to photographs appear in *italic* type.

vanilla bean: Cilantro–Vanilla Bean Dessert Oil, 179, 188, **235**; paste, 179, 235; seeds, 235; where to buy, 238

vanilla extract, 179, 182, 185, 190, 193–95, 197, 207, 235

vegan recipe, 84

vegetable oil, 17, 25, 30, 73, 89, 94, 95, 122, 137, 163, 165

vegetable stock: any vegetable stock, 82–84, 226; Best Vegetable Stock, 62, 65, **68**, 69, 226, 229

vegetarian recipes, 77, 80, 83

venison, 128, 143, 147; Dark Stock (bison, lamb, venison), 141, **143**, 144; Loretta's Big Biscuits with Sausage Gravy, **147**, 157; Venison Shank Braised with Juniper and Sage, 128

vinaigrette: Balsamic

Vinaigrette, for Tomato and Corn Salad, **41**; Chipotle Vinaigrette, **42**; Cranberry Vinaigrette, *48*, **49**; for Pineapple, Jicama, and Avocado Salad, 40; Spicy Vinaigrette, **51**; Sweet Corn Vinaigrette, **50**, 93; for Three Sisters and Friends Salad, **36**

vinegar, 160; balsamic, 41, 110, 120, 227, 229, 237; cider, 55, 216; pineapple or banana, 51; red wine, 222; rice, 36, 40, 215; rice wine, 49, 109, 226; where to buy, 237–38; white, 197; white wine, 54

walnuts, 61, 83, 163, 170, 197, 237–38; Black Walnut Bread, **170**, *171*; Pralines, **197**; where to buy, 238

wasna, 50; about, 139

watercress, 49, 120; about, *46*, 47

watermelons, 57, 59; Watermelon Gazpacho, **59**

White Bean Hummus, **18**

wild rice: about, 38; how to prepare, 38; as ingredient, 36, 83–84, 146; serve with, 93, 105, 229; where to buy, 238; Wild Rice, Quinoa, and Cranberry Stuffed Squash, **83**

wine: red, 128, 135, 141; white, 82, 99, 101, 105, 114

Worcestershire sauce, 140

yeast, 168, 170, 180

zucchini, 28, 62, 146, 215; Three Sisters and Friends Salad, **36**, *37*, 167; Three Sisters Sauté with Sage Pesto, **28**, *29*